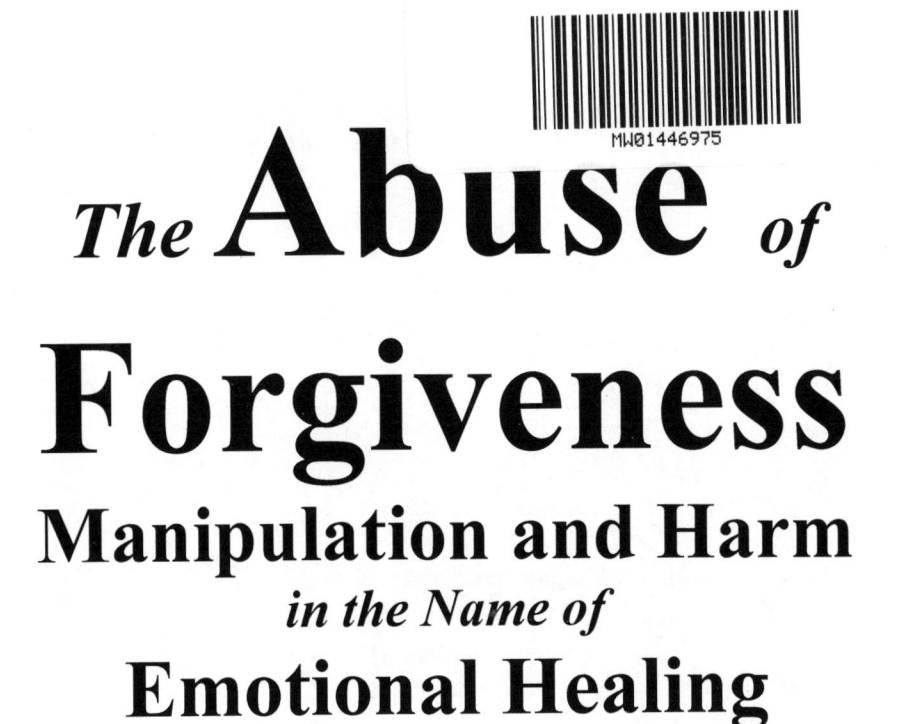

The Abuse of Forgiveness

Manipulation and Harm
in the Name of
Emotional Healing

Umm Zakiyyah

The Abuse of Forgiveness: Manipulation and Harm in the Name of Emotional Healing
By Umm Zakiyyah

Copyright © 2017 by Al-Walaa Publications.
All Rights Reserved.

ISBN: 978-1-942985-13-6
Library of Congress Control Number: 2017949033

Order information at uzauthor.com/bookstore

Verses from Qur'an adapted from Saheeh International, Darussalam, and Yusuf Ali translations.

Published by Al-Walaa Publications
Camp Springs, Maryland USA

Cover photo from Shutterstock.com © by Numpon Jumroonsiri

Table of Contents

Glossary of Arabic Terms	4
Foreword	5
1. The Death of Forgiveness	9
2. Forced Forgiveness	13
3. You Don't Matter: The First Rule of Forced Forgiveness	16
4. Not Forgiving Isn't Unforgiving	19
5. What Is Forgiveness Exactly?	22
6. When Forgiveness Isn't Forgiveness	29
7. Anger and Bitterness in Abuse Survivors	38
8. Distinguishing Faith from Forgiveness	47
9. Success and Sincerity in Forced Forgiveness	51
10. The Gift of Not Forgiving	55
11. Self Deception in Forgiveness Culture	60
12. But Doesn't God Love Forgiveness?	65
13. Why Forgiveness Isn't For Everyone	71
14. Toxic Negativity in Extreme Positivity	79
15. Good Anger, Bad Anger	90
16. Reclaiming the Beauty of Forgiveness	96
17. When To Encourage Forgiveness	104
Final Notes	109
Also By Umm Zakiyyah	110
About the Author	111
References	112

Glossary of Arabic Terms

Allah: Arabic word for "God" but most specifically "the only One who has the right to be worshipped"

'aqeedah: core beliefs that define a person's spiritual outlook and path in life

dhulm: wrongdoing or oppression

du'aa: informal prayerful supplication

emaan: sincere and authentic spirituality rooted in proper faith or belief in God

fitrah: the human's inherent perfect spiritual nature that is inclined toward authentic spirituality (humbly and sincerely worshipping and obeying Allah alone)

hadd: legal or worldly punishment for a crime

ikhlaas: spiritual sincerity; pure God-centered intention rooted in the heart-spirit-soul of the believer and inspires all outward words and actions that reflect true *emaan* (authentic spirituality)

insha'Allah: God-willing

jihaad-al-nafs: the ongoing internal battle of the spirit-soul against itself for the goal of continuous spiritual purity throughout life

madhloom: victim/survivor of wrongdoing or oppression

qadr: predestination; divine decree; the past, present, and future that is already divinely determined and written for every individual

sabeel: road, pathway, or course of action or behavior

sabr: patience rooted in spiritual sincerity and perseverance upon authentic spirituality

Salaah: formal obligatory five daily prayers for Muslims

Shaytaan: Satan; devil

shirk: assigning divine attributes to creation or creation's attributes to God; giving to creation any rights that are solely for God; worshipping anything or anyone along with or instead of God; paganism or idol worship

shukr: sincere gratefulness to God

tafseer: explanations of the meanings of Qur'an

tawakkul: full and sincere trust in God

Foreword

◆

This book came about as part of my own healing journey. As I continuously sought healing from my own emotional trauma, I found myself constantly re-triggered by popular notions of forgiveness, specifically the idea that my own healing could not even *begin* until I forgave those who wronged me. If I voiced even the option to not forgive, I was immediately assaulted with guilt trips that either insinuated or outright claimed that I was angry, bitter, and unforgiving. Sometimes the person claimed that my even speaking about not forgiving indicated a sick heart, a character flaw, or a complete disconnect from the love and pleasure of God. Usually these attacks were issued through emotional and spiritual manipulation inquiries like, "What kind of person would not forgive the one who wronged them?"

As many of my readers know, I am Muslim and often write about the spiritual struggles of Muslims, as well as about Muslim-Christian interfaith in America. In this book, I tackle a topic that extends far beyond religion as practiced in faith communities and reaches into emotional healing, mental health, life coaching, and self-help: forgiveness as it is popularly understood and pushed today.

Undoubtedly, when forgiveness is offered from a place of unfettered choice rooted in a sincere heart seeking spiritual height, it is a beautiful, rewarding, and powerful experience. However, when it is offered due to being guilted into believing that it is a condition of one's own emotional healing and personal growth, it becomes a tool of manipulation and harm, regardless of the good intentions of the one pushing forgiveness as the price of emotional health and inherent goodness.

When the victim of forgiveness peddling (or "forced forgiveness") is a survivor of emotional trauma incited by some form of abuse—whether physical, sexual, verbal, emotional, or any other—the process of offering this forced forgiveness can become a form of emotional injury itself, as well as a consistent trigger of the original abuse. When God is used as the central "voice" in the guilting, forgiveness peddling can fall into the category of spiritual abuse.

Naturally, sometimes this forced forgiveness is well-meaning and pushed with good intentions. Other times it is intentionally manipulative and self-serving, especially when coming from the abusers or wrongdoers themselves (or their supporters and enablers). Either way, the result is the same: harm and re-wounding to the survivors of the initial trauma.

Because faith communities are often at the forefront in pushing forced forgiveness, in this book, I discuss some spiritual concepts from my faith tradition. At times, these concepts will overlap Judeo-Christian traditions, at other times they will not. However, I believe that these spiritual reflections can be helpful to anyone seeking relief from the shackles of forced forgiveness, even if the person does not ascribe to any faith tradition.

In a book of this nature, I think it is important to emphasize that faith communities are not the only ones using forgiveness as a tool of manipulation and harm. In nearly all communities, we have a growing group of abused and traumatized individuals who need healing from "forgiveness" itself.

I want to also point out that I am not a mental health expert. I am merely a survivor of emotional trauma who has sought help from multiple sources on my healing journey. At times this journey has been very painful, and at times it has been very empowering. Naturally, there are aspects of emotional healing that are inherently painful. But what I discovered was that some advice and direction I received only exacerbated that pain and re-traumatized me, and some propelled me forward on the path to healing. By far, of the most damaging advice and direction I received came from those who continuously pushed forgiveness as a condition of healing.

In this book, I share what I learned about this abuse of forgiveness and why I believe it must stop. I also share what I, as well as other survivors and some mental health experts, say is the proper way to understand forgiveness in light of emotional healing. For sure, manipulation and harm have no place in the healing process, and especially not from those trusted with aiding survivors on this journey.

Forgiveness is a beautiful thing. I hope through this book that we are reminded of what it truly means so that we can return to offering it from a place of sincerity instead of coercion. I also hope that we come to understand that forgiveness is not a condition of emotional healing, no matter how much we are convinced otherwise. Yes, forgiveness might have meant emotional healing for *you*, and I wouldn't even attempt to deny that because you know your truth better than anyone else.

But you do not know my truth or anyone else's. And I can attest to the fact that toxic anger and bitterness are not always on the other side of not forgiving. Furthermore, it is my belief that anyone who truly understands the meaning of forgiveness would not voluntarily put themselves in a position of harming someone emotionally (and thus need forgiveness themselves). And that's precisely what we are doing when we tell survivors of abuse and wrongdoing that forgiveness is a condition of their emotional wellbeing and personal growth, thereby overstepping our bounds and potentially participating in a subtle form of abuse.

If that sounds a bit shocking or troubling because you genuinely believe you are helping survivors, not hurting them, when you push them to forgive their abusers, then this book is for you. And I encourage every well-meaning advisor and supporter of any survivor—whether you are a friend, loved one, religious leader, life coach or mental health expert—to consider what I say with an open mind and heart. The emotional health and wellbeing of the survivor who trusts you (or even the very relationship you enjoy) could depend on it.

"People start to heal the moment they feel heard."
—Cheryl Richardson

*"Today I focus on neither blame nor forgiveness regarding those who have hurt me. I focus on only healing.
And I leave it to God to take account of their deeds."*
—from the journal of Umm Zakiyyah

1
The Death of Forgiveness

"For trauma survivors, there are many paths to healing and moving on. Why does forgiveness culture demand that survivors forgive their abusers?"
—Elizabeth Switaj, "Why I Reject Forgiveness Culture"

I wanted to die. I *needed* to die.

These thoughts swam around in my mind until they gripped my consciousness and became *me*. I lay on my side motionless, my limbs weakened, my head pounding. The feather mattress beneath me offered little comfort in the darkness that was suffocating me under the glow of sunshine that illuminated my bedroom through the blinds. I stared off into the distance at nothing in particular and knew with certainty that the world would be better off without me.

I thought of the painkillers in the medicine cabinet in the bathroom across the hall. *How many should I take to end my life?* I wondered, the question more practical than dismal.

Are you crazy? another voice immediately berated me. It was coming from the far recesses of my mind. Though it was more distant than the one saying that I should down the pills, it was rooted in the panicked frenzy of my soul. There, beneath my calloused heart, was a trace of *emaan*. It was like dust settled upon a forgotten shelf, where I'd long since stashed my faithful self.

Do you want to follow up hell in this life with worse hell in the next? Like air drifting in from a corridor in the moment between the quick opening and shutting of a door, the question stirred the settled dust only barely. But my answer was discernable nonetheless. *No, I do not.* It was a whisper of an answer, but it woke some of the dormant faith within me.

You have no right to live anymore, a more authoritative voice countered the weak attempts at fending for my soul. *Look at how many people you are burdening with your existence.*

Fortunately, I survived this ordeal unscathed, but the memory remains raw and chilling. I'd never before experienced such a harrowing internal battle for my life. About a year after this fateful fight, I happened upon this entry in my personal journal: *I'm sorry. I didn't mean to exist. I swear, I had nothing to do with it.* Tears filled my eyes as I got choked up reliving that moment at the sight of those words.

I mention this heartbreaking memory because surviving this ordeal was one of many significant events that marked for me the death of living in servitude to manipulation and harm, and the beginning of living in commitment to emotional and spiritual healing—sans forced forgiveness. Choosing to live life on my terms was for me one of the final stages of agonizing labor before giving birth to my "self."

Shortly before this life altering moment, I had quit my fulltime job due to having inexplicable health struggles. I would wake up with splitting headaches and numbness in my arms and legs. Unable to walk without support, I would press my palms against the wall and slowly steady myself as I made my way to the bathroom to shower and get dressed. At work, exhaustion would overtake me until I feared my head would literally drop on the keyboard at my desk. Sometimes part of my vision would go and I'd be unable to see the entire computer monitor. At home, I would periodically feel faint all of a sudden and have to steady myself on nearby furniture to resist a fall.

"What is going on with you?" my doctor said as she reviewed the results of my recent tests. I could tell by the way she asked the question that she knew that my problems were far deeper than blood results and physiology. She advised me to reduce all stress and to avoid taxing my mind and body unnecessarily, no matter how harmless a task seemed to me. I then was told that until I rebuilt my health, I should no longer participate in fasting.

This was a wake-up call for me, as I'd genuinely had no idea that things had gotten this bad. I had been experiencing migraines for years, but I just chalked it up to my personal fate. It wasn't until my husband pointed out the timing of my most debilitating migraines and body weakness that I realized the answer to my doctor's question: I was continuously inciting debilitating stress by "dutifully" interacting with friends and loved ones who'd repeatedly caused me harm.

I didn't mention to my husband my recent close call with suicide. I was too shaken, afraid, and humiliated to face what this recollection would mean if I got up the nerve to confess it aloud. But deep inside, the lure and "need" still lurked, and this terrified me. I needed help, but I had no idea how to ask for it, or get it.

I already felt like my existence was a burden to the world, hence the dark temptation to end it all. What would happen if I became a burden to my husband too? Surely, he didn't sign up for this. The realization of the possibility of losing his confidence and trust sent my mind and heart into a panicked frenzy. I couldn't chance overburdening him with something as dismal as this. He was all I had for emotional support. If I told him and he couldn't handle it, then I'd have no one. At the same time, I couldn't chance *not* getting help—if I were to remain alive and sane.

What could I do?

As I listened to my husband recount all the times I'd lain immobile in bed afflicted with migraines and unable to fully walk, I realized what I had to do. It became clear, beyond a shadow of a doubt, that my emotional and mental health (and perhaps my physical life itself) depended on two things: One, cutting all toxic relationships from my life, irrespective of whether we were bonded through friendship, faith, or blood. Two, getting professional help however and wherever I could.

At the time, I didn't view moving forward with this decision as related to forgiveness at all. I didn't even fully comprehend what moving forward would mean. I just knew I couldn't continue fighting my internal battles alone.

Throughout the course of my healing journey, I would be confronted with the concept of forgiveness over and over again. Initially, the encounters did not faze me, as in my mind they were unrelated to my emotional wounds. Eventually, however, these encounters (which were increasingly frequent) became annoying, frustrating, and finally, triggering.

The experience of becoming physically sick and distressed in discussions of forgiveness forced me to explore what was happening with me. I couldn't understand why the topic of forgiveness continuously incited faintness, migraines, and body weakness. These were the same reactions I had to interacting with the people who inflicted the initial wounding, and they were the same reactions I had to facing circumstances that mirrored that wounding in some way.

But why was the topic of forgiveness triggering?

As I sought healing from both emotional trauma and the consistent retriggering in cultures of forced forgiveness, I began to understand forgiveness in an entirely new light, emotionally and spiritually. Thus, for me, my determination to live and heal after feeling I must die marked the beginning of the death of forgiveness as I naively understood the concept at the time.

2
Forced Forgiveness

"In a culture that stigmatizes those who refuse to forgive, the added stress can lead to poorer health and slower recovery."
—Elizabeth Switaj, "Why I Reject Forgiveness Culture"

◆

"I don't know why you'd want to live with all that anger and bitterness!" a woman said in response to a survivor who'd expressed that she wasn't going to forgive her abuser. We were all part of an online group established for sharing inspiring stories about overcoming difficulty and supporting each other on our emotional healing journeys. Watching the exchange, I was tempted to chime in and share my point of view. But I said nothing, my heart telling me that it was best to leave it alone. I already knew how most of these discussions ended: with a forgiveness peddler using emotional manipulation to guilt a survivor into forgiving his or her abuser. In other words, most of these discussions ended exactly how this one had begun.

Previously on other forums, I had attempted to explain how a person could choose not to forgive yet let go of anger and bitterness, heal fully, and live an emotionally healthy and fulfilling life. But the forgiveness peddlers would hear nothing of it. No one's healing was real except their own. I sometimes spent a considerable amount of time breaking down the definition of forgiveness and contrasting it with the definition of healing to show how one was not a condition of the other. Yet still, even after they admitted to understanding what I was saying, forced forgiveness zealots would return to their tactic of emotional manipulation to insist that anyone who chose not to forgive was suffering from a corrupt heart.

Repeatedly observing these attacks on survivors who had chosen not to forgive made it clear to me that the culture of forced forgiveness was much more widespread and destructive than I'd initially fathomed. And it wasn't just fellow survivors participating in the emotional manipulation. There were life coaches, religious leaders, and even mental health professionals.

Being repeatedly exposed to the hostile environment of forced forgiveness was very similar to what I often experienced from anti-religion zealots who insisted that anyone who believed in God and affiliated with organized religion—especially Islam—was either evil themselves or a passive participant in evil. This misguided conviction gave them license to mock, harass, and slander Jews, Christians, and Muslims at every opportunity, then say to them, "If you want to make the world a peaceful, loving place, then stop worshipping that fake God of yours!" In this, they failed to realize that they themselves were demonstrating the very opposite of the peace, love, and compassion they claimed to desire for the world.

I mention the hostility of anti-religion zealots because the environment of forced forgiveness mirrors it in many ways. In the word *forgiveness*, we have a phenomenal concept rooted in spreading peace, love, and compassion. However, in the culture of forced forgiveness, the tactics being used to spread this beautiful concept are anything but peaceful, loving, or compassionate. How then can we truly achieve peace, love, and compassion—within ourselves or the world—if we cannot first display these traits in our speech and actions? Moreover, what do we even imagine peace, love, and compassion actually mean if we cannot accept that someone else's path toward them could look a bit different from ours?

Forced Forgiveness

In the context of this book, I define *forced forgiveness* as any guilting, demand, or pressure to forgive that inextricably links the survivor's emotional healing, personal growth, mental health, or spiritual goodness to forgiving the one(s) who inflicted the emotional wounding. I use the term *forgiveness peddling* (or *peddling forgiveness*) to refer to the effective "selling" of forgiveness by any trusted advisor, mental health expert, or spiritual leader as the only path to emotional healing for a survivor.

I define *false forgiveness* as the survivor's premature decision to forgive an abuser or wrongdoer as a result of being guilted, demanded, or pressured to forgive under the misguided assumption that forgiving is a prerequisite to their emotional healing (or that it equals emotional healing).

Both forgiveness peddling and a survivor's subsequent false forgiveness allow the advisors, experts, and leaders who are engaged in forced forgiveness to operate under the illusion that they have successfully done their job in guiding a person toward emotional healing. However, in reality, all they have done is circumvent, trivialize, or deny the real work involved in emotional healing, work that is neither increased nor decreased based on the survivor's decision to forgive (or not). Furthermore, forgiveness peddling robs the survivor of his or her right to personal choice and to receiving meaningful help on the journey toward emotional healing, which has nothing whatsoever to do with the abusers themselves. Most tragically, forced forgiveness often becomes a subtle form of abuse or trauma itself.

3
You Don't Matter
The First Rule of Forced Forgiveness

"Real forgiveness is most commonly found in the calm eye of the hurricane of blame."
—Pete Walker, *The Tao of Fully Feeling*

◆

Ironically, when I found myself the repeated recipient of forgiveness peddling, I had already forgiven the ones who had wronged me. As a Muslim, I understood forgiveness as simply the decision to seek no revenge or punishment for the person in this life or the Hereafter as a result of being wronged. In making this voluntary decision, I opened up for myself the opportunity to even *greater* reward for my suffering, as I was already promised recompense from God due to being unjustly harmed in the first place. I knew I had full rights to *not* forgive, and I didn't imagine that my decision in either direction had anything at all to do with who I was as a human being, personally or spiritually.

It was during my journey toward healing following my close call with suicide that I encountered forgiveness peddlers who made me feel like there was something inherently evil about me. Even as I had already forgiven those who harmed me, the forgiveness peddlers effectively told me that my depression, physical ailments, and mental suffering in the face of triggers were due to my refusal to forgive the ones who had afflicted the emotional wounds.

This claim confused me, as I hadn't even vocalized to them that I either forgave or didn't forgive the ones who had harmed me. Why then did I keep hearing about the necessity of forgiveness when I had already forgiven?

If you're still hurting, then you haven't truly forgiven. This would be the answer I ultimately received—over and over again.

Hearing this demoralizing message while seeking some

semblance of hope after feeling like I was a bad person and a burden to everyone I loved and cared for was dangerously traumatic. It sent me into deep confusion and self-doubt, and I wondered if in fact there was something inherently evil about me.

If even my decision to forgive was ineffective and self-destructive, what did that say about me as a person? Was there any hope for me? Was I so wicked and insincere that God himself was punishing me by afflicting me with continuous mental, emotional, and physical distress?

Naturally, feeling spiritually corrupt, evil, and incorrigible sent me right back into the dark place I had been trying to escape when I'd sought help from my emotional suffering in the first place. Consequently, I repeatedly found myself fighting thoughts that I was better off dead.

Do I Even Matter Here?

In time, I would grow accustomed to the oft-repeated message that I now understand as the first rule of forced forgiveness: *You don't matter*. Interestingly, this rule is also the underlying ideology of all abuse itself, hence the title of the book, *The Abuse of Forgiveness*.

Forced forgiveness teaches us that our wholeness as human beings—and thus our entire existence—is inextricably linked to the sins of those who have wronged, abused, or traumatized us. To understand this puzzling, destructive ideology, I offer the following analogy about a victim of a burglary and destruction of property.

Being the recipient of forced forgiveness is like someone having their most precious belongings stolen from them such that their entire life is turned upside down. They have no bed to sleep on, no clothes to wear, no food to eat, and only the crumbling walls of a home that doesn't even protect them from the heat or cold. When they ask what they can do to start over, they're told to use whatever resources they have to give gifts to the thieves. And each time they ask a practical question about restocking what they lost, they're told to find the thieves and give them whatever they have. If they refuse, they're told, "You're still living like this because you're stingy and greedy in refusing to share with the thieves!"

In the language of religion, forced forgiveness teaches us that God punishes us for suffering abuse. It teaches us that our greatest sin is to feel the pain of our wounds and to feel upset at the ones who inflicted them. It further teaches us that God will decree that we live with corrupt, angry, bitter hearts until we no longer feel or acknowledge the pain of our wounds—or until we no longer feel any frustration or blame toward those who hurt us.

Tragically, the underlying message of forced forgiveness is that mercy and forgiveness are automatic and unconditional for abusers and transgressors, but they are delayed and conditional for the sufferers of abuse and wrongdoing. Moreover, it teaches us that an extra level of punishment from God is inflicted on the sufferers of abuse if they should place any delays or conditions on showing mercy and forgiveness to wrongdoers. In other words, from both the healing and religious perspective, forced forgiveness teaches us that sufferers of abuse don't matter; only the abusers do.

4

Not Forgiving Isn't Unforgiving

"When we advise people to forgive and move on, we may make things worse."
—David Bedrick, "6 Reasons Not To Forgive, Not Yet"

◆

In discussing the manipulation and harm that abuse survivors often face from those who equate forgiveness with emotional healing, I think it is crucial to make an important distinction: Choosing not to forgive someone is *not* the same as being unforgiving. The former is merely exercising one's right to choice, and the latter is a negative character trait. In practical reality, only the latter generally stems from a corrupt, angry, bitter heart. And the one has absolutely nothing to do with the other, as not forgiving is in no way related to being unforgiving.

In the context of religion, when we are advised by God to pardon and forgive others as a general rule, we are being advised to have a generally forgiving nature—and we are being cautioned against corrupting our hearts with toxic anger and bitterness toward others. We are also being taught to generally seek peace and reconciliation amongst ourselves, and to generally be facilitators of peace and reconciliation when we find others fighting or showing animosity toward one another.

Even God Himself—who is Most Merciful, Loving, and All-Forgiving (and in a manner that supersedes the compassion of humans)—has things that He does not forgive. In Islamic tradition, all sins have the opportunity to be forgiven except one: dying upon *shirk* or disbelief after having known full well on earth one's spiritual duty to worship and serve God alone. However, while someone is still alive, even *shirk* and disbelief are forgiven by God if one repents and mends his or her ways before death. For all other sins, God looks at the heart and soul of each person and calls them to account one by one on the Day of Judgment. Some sins will be forgiven. Others will not.

When God in His infinite knowledge, justice, and wisdom decides to punish someone for their sins, no person of faith would describe Him as "unforgiving." However, when God in His infinite knowledge, justice, and wisdom decides to give survivors choice in forgiving or not forgiving their abusers, we call survivors angry, bitter and "unforgiving" if they choose the latter.

Why?

In light of the fact that our Most Merciful, Loving, and Forgiving God is the one who gave survivors the right to *not* forgive, if there is anyone with corruption in their minds and hearts, it is the person who harasses and abuses survivors in the name of forgiveness.

Forgiving, Unforgiving, and Not Forgiving

People who have a forgiving nature are known to do the following as a general rule: avoid holding grudges, pardon minor foibles, overlook faults, make excuses for people, accept apologies for minor wrongs, assume the best about others, and interpret actions or situations in their best light.

People whose character is unforgiving are known to do the following as a general rule: easily and quickly hold grudges, seek revenge for even minor slights, find fault in others, refuse to make amends, assume the worst about others, and interpret ambiguous statements and behavior negatively. Unforgiving people are generally spiteful, vengeful and view even the slightest mistake as a cause to hold a grudge and avenge the wrong.

Here, I think it is important to distinguish between the actions and interpretations of events by those suffering from mental illness or emotional trauma and triggers rooted in complex PTSD (post traumatic stress disorder), and people who are unforgiving. Though this topic is far too vast for the purpose of this book, an overly simplistic difference between the two is this: Those suffering from mental illness or PTSD are reacting to a very "real" threat of harm that the mind has exaggerated in a manner that is beyond their control, and those who are unforgiving have made the conscious choice to exaggerate the harm of a situation due to their toxic pride, anger, or bitterness.

In contrast to being unforgiving, choosing to not forgive someone is simply a decision to heal and move forward in a manner that does not absolve the abuser or wrongdoer in any way. Not forgiving someone does not necessarily involve unhealthy anger or bitterness, and it does not necessarily reflect spiritual corruption in any form. In fact, for some people, deeper healing and increased spirituality are achieved through *not* forgiving the wrongdoer.

5
What Is Forgiveness Exactly?

"You can't dictate what forgiving and letting go of hurt looks like for someone else."
—excerpt of *PAIN. From the Journal of Umm Zakiyyah*

As I continuously faced forgiveness peddlers who effectively told me that I was a bitter, spiritually devolved person because I didn't feel I *had* to forgive in order to heal, I came to a realization. The way I understood forgiveness was not the way that they understood forgiveness. While I certainly recognize the phenomenal power of forgiveness in its own right, I began to understand that the culture of forced forgiveness had robbed the term of its magnificent, luminous qualities and put in its place a tool of manipulation and harm—just as abusers and emotional manipulators had done with the term *love*.

Part of the reason that forced forgiveness has inflicted so much emotional wounding, even as it has indeed inspired ostensible healing, is that the word *forgiveness* itself has taken on a life of its own. In forgiveness culture as it is practiced today, sometimes forgiveness means actual forgiveness, and sometimes it means something else entirely. Oddly, many who are at the forefront of insisting that forgiveness is the "cure all" to survivors of trauma do not have a clear idea of what the word actually means—to themselves or others. However, most forgiveness peddlers have a pretty clear idea regarding what they imagine it actually *does* (i.e. heal emotional trauma), which is why they push it so relentlessly and insist that it is *the* antidote for healing from abuse and wrongdoing.

Some forgiveness peddlers have a clear idea of what *they* mean by forgiveness, but then erroneously (and sometimes arrogantly) project their definition onto others. When they guilt, demand, or pressure others to forgive in the name of healing, what they fail to realize is that the recipient of the advice might understand the term in a completely different way. As such, even if the survivor were to implement the advice, forgiveness often cannot (and does not) produce the desired result (i.e. emotional healing).

Like discussions of *love* in abusive, toxic and dysfunctional families and relationships, discussions of *forgiveness* have become convoluted, ambiguous, contradictory, confusing, and even damaging when linked inextricably to emotional healing. And like love, forgiveness is declared and encouraged much more than it is clearly defined and understood.

Most seriously, even when forgiveness is clearly defined by the one speaking about it, it is very rare that the speaker shows compassion and empathy toward the one he or she is speaking to—except to display obligatory patience with the hurt that the person is feeling, while "humbly" insisting that the person will one day "come around" to be freed from the anger and bitterness that (allegedly) binds them to their wounds.

In this, forgiveness peddlers fail to realize the high possibility that it is they who are less emotionally evolved than the survivor who has chosen not to forgive. In many cases, the survivor is merely emotionally mature and spiritually intelligent enough to realize that his or her emotional wellbeing is in no way connected to the abuser or wrongdoer. Survivors who have both healed *and* chosen not to forgive their abuser have merely embraced their right to human choice. Their hearts are no more fettered to anger and bitterness than those who peddle forgiveness as the cure to those very ailments.

Moreover, many survivors are merely "fully feeling" individuals, as author Pete Walker would describe them, who embrace their full range of natural human emotions and feelings. These include pain, sadness, and even anger, as *none* of these should be cast away completely in a mentally and emotionally healthy individual.

The problem with many forgiveness peddlers is that they link all emotional healing to having a heart completely free of "negativity." As such, they imagine that any experience or expression of negative feelings means you are a negative, bitter person. This view is similar to their assumption that the act of not forgiving makes a person "unforgiving."

For this reason, it is sometimes the survivor who hasn't forgiven the abuser who is more emotionally evolved than the advisor who insists that forgiveness is the only path to healing. All anger and blame do not equal bitterness, as some experience with and expression of these—even after healing from abuse—merely reflect healthy acceptance of one's authentic human feelings, and the freedom to embrace all of them.

Ironically, it is often the practitioners of forced forgiveness who are most bound to toxic anger and bitterness. Their forbidding themselves the expression of these emotions in their healthy forms most likely means they have not purged them from their heart in their toxic forms. Thus, what they are really feeling is not a heart free of anger and bitterness, but a soul trapped in denial and suppression. This denial and suppression is masked by positive words and external behaviors that mimic gratefulness, love, and forgiveness—as the culture of forced forgiveness demands.

Unfortunately, forced forgiveness has produced a dysfunctional forgiveness culture wherein so many of us have become expert pretenders, and the ones whom we fool most are ourselves. As a result, we have droves of humans who have ostensibly forgiven everyone who has hurt or wronged them, but they deny their own healthy feelings if they are not one hundred percent positive and free of apparent anger and blame.

In his book *The Tao of Fully Feeling*, author Pete Walker aptly describes this dysfunctional aspect of forgiveness culture today when he says, "Most experts on forgiveness seem to be oblivious to the differences between healthy and dysfunctional blame" (2015).

Dictionary Definition of Forgiveness

Merriam-Webster defines *forgive* as the following:
- to give up resentment of or claim to requital
  - *forgive an insult*
- to grant relief from payment of
  - *forgive a debt*

- to cease to feel resentment against (an offender): pardon
  ➤ *forgive one's enemies*

Thus, even from a linguistic, literal standpoint, there are different meanings of *forgiveness*. In the first meaning, it is either an internal experience *or* an external experience. In the second meaning, it is *only* an external experience. In the third meaning, it is not only the internal experience (as discussed in the first definition), but also the cessation of *feeling* the internal experience.

Spiritual Definition of Forgiveness

What all the dictionary definitions of *forgiveness* have in common is that they deal only with the worldly realm of human existence and experience—for both the one granting forgiveness and the one being forgiven. However, as it is understood by those who believe in God and in humanity's ultimate entry into Paradise or Hellfire, forgiveness is essentially a spiritual experience, and it is rooted in the Hereafter and granted solely by God. Thus, for many people of faith, any worldly use of the term *forgiveness* is merely a reflection or extension of this foundational spiritual understanding.

In the spiritual understanding of the term, forgiveness is God's divine decision to suspend a human's deserved punishment in the Hereafter for a sin (or set of sins) committed in the world. While the spiritual definition of forgiveness is rooted in humanity's accountability to God in the Hereafter, what humans are actually accountable for in the afterlife is rooted entirely in how they lived out their lives in this world. Thus, their accountability before God is rooted in their worldly experience, both internally and externally (small aspects of which were discussed in the dictionary definitions of forgiveness).

Nevertheless, this accountability in front of God in the Hereafter includes humans' accountability to each other in the world. As such, an aspect of the spiritual understanding of God's forgiveness includes the worldly understanding of human forgiveness.

For example, in all major faith traditions, humans are required to respect their brothers and sisters in humanity with whom they share the earth. For this reason, following rules that prohibit stealing, killing, lying, slandering, and so on are essential to authentic faith practice.

In Islamic tradition, any disobedience to God is by definition *dhulm*—wrongdoing or oppression—and every *dhulm* has the threat of punishment in the Hereafter. This *dhulm* is manifested in two possible behavior types: wronging oneself or wronging others. Both are forbidden and thus can subject a person to punishment in the Hereafter. Punishment in the afterlife includes one or more of the following: torment in the grave, torment on the Day of Judgment, and/or torment in Hellfire.

Generally speaking, the first type of *dhulm* behavior harms only oneself while the second type harms both oneself and others. Although all sin falls under the category of *dhulm* and thus brings potential harm upon the wrongdoer's soul in the Hereafter, the second type of *dhulm* (wronging others) exacerbates that self harm in that it multiplies the wrongdoer's sins and supplants an added barrier to God's forgiveness.

For the generally sinful (i.e. those who have wronged only themselves), there is only the single barrier of the necessity of sincere repentance in the world as a condition of God's forgiveness. However, for the sinful who have transgressed the rights of someone else, there is the added barrier of the victim being granted the right to demand full requital for the wrong—in addition to the necessity of the wrongdoer sincerely repenting to God.

Spiritually speaking, this means that the abuser or wrongdoer has two levels of punishment: one from the victim of the wrongdoing, and the other from God. Additionally, in Islamic tradition, a person who has wronged someone is not forgiven by God until the victim of the wrongdoing first forgives the person.

Depending on the type of abuse or wrongdoing, there may be the added level of *hadd* or worldly punishment. For example, a major sin like murder is considered both a legal and spiritual crime in Islamic tradition. In this crime of murder, the surviving loved ones can decide whether or not to demand legal punishment for the crime. However, the decision of the family to forgo the legal punishment in this world does not necessarily absolve the wrongdoer of punishment in front of God in the Hereafter.

In contrast, a sin like backbiting (i.e. saying anything about a person that they would dislike) is not a legal crime in Islamic tradition, but it is a spiritual crime. As such, the victim of the backbiting can demand requital in the Hereafter, or they can forgive the *dhulm* such that they forgo any recompense from the backbiter in the afterlife for suffering the wrongdoing.

In all crimes of wrongdoing, even those that do not carry a legal punishment in this world, there is also the worldly recompense of a *du'aa* granted. This *du'aa* is the prayerful supplication of the *madhloom* (the one who has been wronged) in which God will grant the *madhloom* whatever he or she asks of Him. In this, the victim can ask for a specific punishment, humiliation, or torment (whether worldly or spiritual) to befall the abuser or wrongdoer; and God promises that He will grant it.

In Islamic tradition, spiritual recompense for having suffered abuse or wrongdoing also includes the wrongdoer coming on the Day of Judgment and repaying his or her "debts" to the victim. This means that the good deeds on the wrongdoer's scale are transferred to the victim. If the wrongdoer runs out of good deeds in the process, then the sins that the victim committed in the world are piled upon the scale of the wrongdoer until the "debt" between them in settled. Then the wrongdoer enters the Hellfire.

Therefore, when understanding the concept of forgiveness in light of one human wronging another, there is worldly forgiveness, and there is Hereafter forgiveness. Worldly forgiveness simply entails the victim voluntarily relinquishing any claims to the wrongdoer being issued either a legal punishment for the crime or a punishment in response to the *du'aa* of the *madhloom*. Hereafter forgiveness simply entails the victim voluntarily relinquishing any claims to spiritual recompense (in the form of the wrongdoer paying for the crimes in the afterlife). However, all forgiveness has the natural spiritual recompense (for the victim) of increased mercy and forgiveness from God.

Whenever a victim forgives a wrongdoer (i.e. voluntarily relinquishes rights to worldly or spiritual requital), God rewards them manifold for this, as this is not something that is required of them. However, under no circumstances does God punish a victim of wrongdoing, even if this "punishment" is merely afflicting their hearts with toxic anger and bitterness until they agree to forgive the wrongs.

6
When Forgiveness Isn't Forgiveness

"If someone wrongs you, then you *are in sin. This is forgiveness culture today."*
—from the journal of Umm Zakiyyah

◆

It is really difficult to work through the emotional and psychological damage of being effectively taught that any *experiencing* of your pain is wronging the one who inflicted it. In this, I'm talking about how I was taught that the *experience* of pain must be filtered through the good intentions of the wrongdoer, particularly if that person is "superior" to me in any way. This superiority could be due to a blood relationship we share, their older numerical age, their higher religious status, or even sociopolitical constructs that deem me a minority.

It was only when—and if—my superiors gave me permission to *feel* the pain they inflicted that I was allowed to exist as a full human being, as part of myself. Without this permission, any signs or expression of pain sustained as a result of their emotional wounding pointed to my mental or spiritual corruption. Or it pointed to my toxic anger or bitterness, which I allegedly suffered as a result of "refusing" to forgive. This is the culture of abuse that I've experienced on many fronts, and it is rooted in making sure the privileged are comfortable and unoffended, even when they're hurting you.

In this dysfunctional aspect of today's forgiveness culture, a survivor of child abuse is reminded that his parents "did the best they could," a survivor of domestic violence is told that her husband loves her and just doesn't know how to show it, a survivor of spiritual abuse is reminded of the superiority of religious scholars, a survivor of abuse by family is told that "blood is thicker than water," and a victim of police violence or racism is told that the aggressors didn't mean to hurt them or their loved ones—or that their own negative traits (even if only imagined by the aggressor) caused the attack. All of this serves as a reminder that to even *express* pain sustained from wounds inflicted by those who are "superior" is a sign of one's self-destructive anger and bitterness and refusal to see the good in people.

In my own healing journey, I began to understand the emotional harm of trying to mitigate pain through reminding myself of the apparent good intentions of the ones who wounded me. This mitigation is especially harmful during the beginning of the healing process when you are first processing the raw anger and blame as a result of what happened. While the consideration of someone's good intentions is not wrong in itself, it should not be used to deny, alleviate, or stop the natural hurt we feel as a result of being harmed, as all wounds inevitably hurt and must be tended to, even if inflicted accidentally.

In my book *Pain. From the Journal of Umm Zakiyyah*, I share this personal reflection, which I wrote as a result of realizing that all my efforts of trying to make excuses for the ones who wounded me only delayed my own healing—and exacerbated my pain: *You can make a million excuses for the one who hurt you, but you'd still have to tend to the wound.*

Forgiveness As Denial

It is enough of a catastrophe that forgiveness culture today is rooted in emotionally manipulating survivors of abuse into forgiving wrongdoers as a prerequisite to their own emotional healing. To make matters worse, much advice regarding healing from abuse by loved ones takes this manipulation a step further by encouraging outright denial of the abuse as the definition of forgiveness itself.

As harmful as the manipulation of forced forgiveness is, if the forgiveness that is ultimately granted is actual forgiveness, at least the survivor has the validation that what she experienced actually happened and is wrong. However, when forgiveness is defined as doubting your own memory, reconstructing the traumatic events to favor the abuser, and understanding all clear harm through the lens of the abuser's good intentions, then the process of "forgiving" merely mirrors aspects of abuse itself, specifically the abusive technique of gaslighting.

In the article "Gaslighting Definition, Techniques and Being Gaslighted," Natasha Tracy defines *gaslighting* as follows:

> Gaslighting is a form of emotional abuse where the abuser manipulates situations repeatedly to trick the victim into distrusting his or her own memory and perceptions. Gaslighting is an insidious form of abuse. It makes victims question the very instincts that they have counted on their whole lives, making them unsure of anything. Gaslighting makes it very likely that victims will believe whatever their abusers tell them regardless as to their own experience of the situation. Gaslighting often precedes other types of emotional and physical abuse because the victim of gaslighting is more likely to remain in other abusive situations as well (May 2016).

Unfortunately, faith communities are often at the forefront of using gaslighting to force forgiveness, especially when a parent, spouse, or family member inflicted the wrong. In this, they erroneously equate honoring one's parents, respecting one's husband or wife, and keeping family ties with guilting survivors into seeing their abusers and traumatic experiences in ways that are inoffensive to parents and loved ones. They sometimes even encourage victims to remain in abusive situations, citing alleged religious obligations of compassion, forgiveness, and "unconditional love."

While seeking positive lessons from painful experiences can indeed be helpful, especially in the latter stages of healing, convincing a survivor to effectively re-remember the traumatic events in a positive light is more harmful than healing. A survivor can fully acknowledge the horrific nature of the events and still glean meaningful lessons from the experience.

In terms of a survivor fulfilling his or her religious duty to abusive parents and family in hopes of obeying God, I discuss this topic in detail in the book <u>*Reverencing the Wombs That Broke You*</u>.

Forgiveness As Fear and Survival

It took me some time to realize that my emotional triggers in environments of forced forgiveness were at least partially due to having lived daily in a culture that taught me that only white people mattered. As an African-American woman, I subconsciously understood that my social acceptance in wider American society, as well as my emotional and physical safety in predominately white environments, depended almost entirely on my filtering all experiences with racism (by myself and other African-Americans) through one of four lens: denying that any racism was involved, blaming the victim (even in cases of murder), acknowledging the wrong but emphasizing the good intentions of the aggressor, or forgiving any aggression, no matter how horrific.

I also subconsciously understood that none of these lens would be applied by American society to *me*. If I were to offend a white person, even if only by responding to a question posed by them regarding my experiences with racism, then I could not and would not be forgiven. In the face of their apparent offense, it was then my job to console them until they felt reassured that I was ever so grateful to them for even asking the question.

If by chance my initial response to their inquiry involved any expression of intense emotion, whether in frustration or anger about my experiences with racism, it was then my job to apologize to them, even if none of my venting was directed at them specifically. If they were mindful enough to ask my forgiveness for any wrongs they had committed, I was required not only to accept their forgiveness, but to eagerly display the most effusive enthusiasm in light of their ostensible contrition—even if I knew full well that their apology would be followed up with absolutely no action to right the wrong (as was almost always the case).

Under no circumstances was I allowed to bring up the topic of racism myself, even if I was experiencing it daily. All discussions of racism required prior approval by white people. This approval was generally granted either by a white person asking my thoughts on the topic, or by a white person facilitating a formal discussion on the topic. The formality of the discussion allowed the topic to be addressed in a distant, scientific manner that neither stated nor implied any specific culpability or accountability of the white people present. In this way, white people could feel "safe" from both me and their guilt, while feeling contented that they were in the frontlines of battling racism, even if the racism they battled was only philosophical and thus disconnected from anti-Black racism in any practical way.

In such environments, I always forgave. I didn't have any other choice. It was either forgive or suffer. I generally chose the former. Because this "forgiveness as fear" had been one of my earliest experiences with forced forgiveness, when I encountered this same mentality in support groups claiming to support emotional healing, I was repeatedly triggered. In these environments of forced forgiveness, I was immediately reminded that I was in danger of suffering if I didn't forgive in the precise way that my "superiors" dictated I must.

Forgiveness As Apathy, Helplessness and Pseudo-Religiosity

For Black people in America, forgiveness has almost never been a choice. It has been a coping mechanism. In the face of horrific events beyond our control, we have repeatedly turned to faith in God to purge from our hearts the natural anger and frustration felt by those who are relentlessly abused but then denied their right to even the acknowledgement of pain that precedes all healing.

Despite all the extensive research on transgenerational trauma, on suffering emotional and psychological abuse, and on being continuously subjected to gaslighting thereafter, the field of mental health largely ignores the fact that Black people's experience with daily racism falls under all three of these categories. Furthermore, whereas most mental health experts emphasize the need to remove oneself from abusive relationships and toxic environments, they fail to address the fact that the sheer ubiquity of modern day racism (which is sometimes overt and sometimes covert) makes this advice largely impossible, especially for "successful" Black people in predominately white work spaces whose very livelihood depends on working everyday in environments of passive aggressive racism that negatively affect their mental, emotional, and even physical health.

To add insult to injury, when Black people make efforts to create organizations, support groups, or awareness campaigns to address these issues amongst themselves, they are accused of living in the past and wanting to create racial division in "post-racial" America. Meanwhile, efforts to spread awareness about the effects of psychological and emotional abuse get loads of media attention and support, so long as racism is not discussed as a form of them. For even in topics concerning their own mental health, Black people aren't allowed to offend white people.

Tragically, under the umbrella of forgiveness, this devaluing mentality is often spread by Black people themselves. However, occasionally, there emerges a Black person who becomes fed up with the culture of forced forgiveness and speaks up vehemently against it publicly. In his article "Black America owes no forgiveness: How Christianity hinders racial justice", Chauncey DeVega says, "Blacks are expected to absolve White America of its crimes. The rules change when the victim happens to be white" (August 2015). He then goes on to share the following:

> On the one-year anniversary of the death of an 18-year-old black teenager named Michael Brown by a (now confessed racist) white police officer named Darren Wilson in Ferguson, Missouri, Brown's mother, Lezley McSpadden, was asked if she forgave Darren Wilson for his cruel and wanton act of legal murder. She told Al Jazeera that she will "never forgive" Darren Wilson and that "he's evil, his acts were devilish."
>
> Her response is unusual. Its candor is refreshing. Lezley McSpadden's truth-telling reveals the full humanity and emotions of black folks, and by doing so defies the norms which demand that when Black Americans suffer they do so stoically, and always in such a way where forgiveness for racist violence is a given, an unearned expectation of White America.
>
> The expectation that black people will always and immediately forgive the violence done to them by the State, or individual white people, is a bizarre and sick American ritual (August 2015).

He goes on to address the role of religion in this forced forgiveness culture:

> The African-American church is also central to the black American ritual of forgiveness...The notion of "Christian forgiveness" as taught by the black church could also be a practical means of self-medication, one designed to stave off existential malaise, and to heal oneself in the face of the quotidian struggles of life under American Apartheid.
>
> Likewise, some used Christianity and the black church to teach passivity and weakness in the face of white terrorism because some great reward supposedly awaits those who suffer on Earth...
>
> The ritual of immediate and expected black forgiveness fulfills the expectations of the White Gaze and the White Racial Frame. A lack of empathy from White America towards Black America is central to the ritual: if white folks could truly feel the pain of black people (and First Nations, Hispanics and Latinos, and other people of color) in these times of meanness, cruelty, and violence, then immediate forgiveness would not be an expectation. Many white Americans actually believe that black people are superhuman, magical, and do not feel pain. This cannot help but to somehow factor into the public ritual of black people saying "I forgive" the violence visited upon them by white cops, paramilitaries, hate mongers, bureaucrats, and the State...
>
> Here, the ritual of African-American forgiveness allows White America absolution and innocence without having to put in the deeds and necessary hard work for true justice, fairness, and equal democracy on both sides of the color line (August 2015).

Not surprisingly (at least for those familiar with the transgenerational cycle of racism), this double standard of forgiveness has roots in the time of the European enslavement of black people. In the first stage of forced forgiveness during this time, black people were forced to become Christians, thereby cutting off any possibility of even hidden beliefs beyond their masters' control. Then they were taught a very Euro-centric, pro-slavery version of their faith, human goodness, and forgiveness.

In the White American version of Christianity, God became a white man and thus their Lord and Savior (literally), and it was Black people's God-mandated duty to serve the White Divine in body and soul. As such, black slavery was ordained by God, and submission to slavery was a Christian duty. Inherent in this religious duty was the obligation to forgive one's enemies (who happened to strongly resemble their Lord and Savoir). Any evidence of discontent, frustration, or anger with one's oppressive circumstances was swiftly punished in the most gruesome of ways. Naturally, the Christian-ness of the violent, white aggressors could not be questioned, as this was against the law of both church and state.

In this stage of forced forgiveness culture, Black people were taught that good Christians were loving, forgiving, and content with their circumstances. In contrast, bad Christians were angry and violent (if they were black) and thus insubordinate to their masters (who were white). Since the white man was god, his wrath upon black people could not and would not be questioned. But it didn't matter, they were told, as any suffering on earth would be rewarded with Heaven in the afterlife for "good Christians."

As a coping mechanism to these egregious conditions, Black people embraced forced forgiveness because it was their only means of physical survival and mental sanity. They learned to appear content, happy, and pleased with even the most degrading of circumstances. As a form of self-encouragement, they kept telling themselves and each other, often from the church pulpit, that they were good people because they chose forgiveness instead of hate. Till today, the stereotype of the "angry black person" serves as a deterrent to Black people acknowledging or expressing hurt, frustration, or pain.

A similar dysfunctional ideology continues today in nearly all abusive environments, irrespective of one's ethnicity or religion. Naturally (and by design), it is oppressive governments, abusers, and wrongdoers who benefit most from this passive, apathetic concept of human goodness and forgiveness. Not surprisingly, this non-aggression and automatic forgiveness is demanded only from those being oppressed and abused—not from those doing the oppressing or abusing. And like the stereotype of the "angry black person," the stereotype of the "angry, bitter person" who suffered abuse serves as a deterrent to abuse survivors embracing their right to both human choice and angry emotions.

Through this self-destructive definition of human goodness and forgiveness, victims are made to feel good about themselves by viewing all negative feelings and emotions as traits of "bad people" and all positive feelings and emotions as traits of "good people." Thus, survivors continuously strive to keep themselves in the latter category, lest they "turn bad" like their abusers.

In this narrow, overly simplistic understanding of good and evil (and of humanity itself), oppressors and abusers are allowed to continuously harm others and subsequently expect automatic forgiveness and absolution. Meanwhile, this dysfunctional forgiveness culture dictates that victims are either required to submit to the abuse and bear it patiently—as Black people are continuously required to do till today (by both church and state), even in the face overt racism and horrific acts of murder. Or, alternatively, survivors are permitted to escape the abuse itself, but they are then required to do absolutely nothing to hold the oppressors and abusers accountable for their abusive behavior—even if only by not forgiving them in their hearts.

7

Anger and Bitterness in Abuse Survivors

"'Why would you want to hold on to all that anger and bitterness?' they say. As if suffering emotional pain is a choice, and as if fully healing is as simple as reciting the magical incantation, 'I forgive them.'"
—from the journal of Umm Zakiyyah

♦

About a year before I felt the urge to take my own life, I was watching the movie *Taken* with my husband. In one scene, there was an auction of women who had been sex trafficked. Droves of wealthy men watched as each traumatized woman, dazed or drugged, was brought to the stage and forced to stand in skimpy clothes while the men pressed a button to put in their bid to purchase them. At the end of the scene, the most "valuable item" was placed before them. She was a young attractive "untouched" virgin whose starting price was the highest of all.

Right after the announcer listed all the qualities of this "rare prize" and the men began eagerly placing their bids, I felt a surge of anger in me. Before I knew what was happening, I raised my voice over the movie and started raging at my husband. As I ranted, there was a small voice in my head trying to reason with me, but I felt powerless to stop the rant. Today, I don't remember what I was saying exactly, but I do recall this part of my outburst: "This is me! This is me! This is how I feel! Now you can see how I feel!"

I can't fully articulate what I meant by all of this and why this scene in particular triggered me so deeply. I was never sex trafficked or sold into prostitution, and my husband certainly didn't treat me like a "rare prize" to be paraded in front of others so they could gawk at me and name their price. He didn't even abuse me at all. So what was all of this about?

That night, after I calmed down, I sat in pensive silence,

confounded by what had occurred. I sensed that something inside me had snapped and that there was no going back. I didn't know what I was escaping or why I was refusing to return to it. But I knew, in the depths of my being, that life as I knew it was over, and this filled me with both hope and melancholic apprehension. I felt myself get choked up until tears filled my eyes. In this emotional reaction, I felt the beginning of grieving for some tremendous loss that my mind couldn't quite grasp.

Several months later, I was in good spirits when a friend asked if I would give my opinion on a newly released song by an independent artist who was known for conscious music. Thinking nothing of the suggestion, I agreed and stopped what I was doing and listened to the track. The soft, entrancing music wafted from the speakers that I'd attached to an iPod, and I heard these words:

Scars.
Some never go away.
Some retrigger the pain...
Will someone help me?
Will someone heal these scars?
Some penetrate my soul.
Forgive me for my wrongs...

I close my heart
I'm just playing a part
So they can't hurt me
I keep them far
I close my heart
I'm just playing the part
So you can't hurt me.
No, you won't hurt me...

By the time the song finished, I was crying so much that I could barely get my words together. The song was "Scars" by Khalil Ismail from his *The Hoping* album, and it was written about a woman who had been sexually abused by her own father. Like the sex trafficking auction scene in *Taken* that had evoked my unexpected angry outburst, my tears and overwhelming emotional reaction to "Scars" made no sense to me. Just as I had never been sex trafficked, I had never been sexually abused.

Understanding Repressed Anger

Repressed anger can be thought of as suppressed or unreleased hurt, frustration, or rage that is now trapped so deeply inside of us that we are no longer conscious of its existence or origins. However, our minds, emotions, and bodies daily suffer as a result of keeping the anger trapped inside. Because hurt, frustration, and anger were meant to be released in non-damaging ways, when they are not, they manifest themselves in ways that harm the person or others.

If the person continues to keep the hurt, frustration, and anger locked inside, they will eventually implode. During emotional implosion, repressed anger is "triggered" and thus finds release in damaging words or actions that are directed at the self and/or others, often in ways incongruent with the present circumstance. However, during emotional triggers, there is generally something in the present circumstance that mirrors the initial hurt in some way, even though the original hurt and its mirrored aspect are unknown to the person because the memory is now subconscious or repressed.

In the article "The Dangers of Repressing Your Anger," author and counselor Tara Springett says:

> If you are like most spiritual people you are trying hard to do the right thing, be kind and, most of all, forgiving... But unfortunately, there is...danger of trying too hard to be kind and this danger is in repressing our anger...
>
> The first symptom resulting from unconscious anger is fatigue... Another very common symptom...is chronic pain. The third big negative symptom resulting from repressed anger is depression.
>
> How come, you may ask, that suppressed anger can cause all these wide-spread problems? The answer is that often fatigue, pain and depression are more acceptable to us than anger...What is the solution to this very real conundrum? Simply expressed, we need to learn to be angry and loving at the same time (nd, belief.net).

Toxic Anger and Bitterness

Undoubtedly, it is indeed *possible* for a victim of wrongdoing and abuse to suffer toxic anger and bitterness, which in turn can harm their mental, emotional, and spiritual health, sometimes severely. However, this toxicity is not the result of choosing not to forgive, it is the result of something much deeper. Perhaps what is responsible for the widespread assumption that not forgiving actually causes toxic anger and bitterness is the cyclical nature of toxic emotional and spiritual states themselves.

For example, it is undeniable that toxic anger and bitterness result in the impossibility (or extreme unlikelihood) of sincere forgiveness being offered in that emotional state. While the inception of this inability (or decreased ability) to forgive isn't necessarily rooted in the isolated decision of a survivor to not forgive a wrong, any unaddressed toxic anger or bitterness in someone inevitably produces only more anger and bitterness. If this toxicity goes untreated for too long, it can produce an unforgiving nature in the person. This corruption of character makes a person constantly angry and bitter, even when there is no apparent cause to be.

Naturally, the traits of an unforgiving nature (which was defined earlier and distinguished from the isolated choice of not forgiving) include holding grudges, seeking revenge, and eagerly awaiting the punishment of an offender or aggressor, even for the slightest and sincerest of errors. If a person with this destructive nature is wronged or treated unjustly, their processing of this wrongdoing, as well as their subsequent response to it, will almost certainly be rooted in the toxic anger and bitterness in which they daily live.

Thus, when this person chooses to not forgive, it almost certainly will result in only increased anger and bitterness. This anger and bitterness stems from the fact that the person is trapped in the cycle of emotional toxicity in which his or her heart is a deadly weapon. It is this personality for whom this popular quote is quite apt: *The one who uses his heart as a weapon must first harm himself.*

What those involved in forced forgiveness fail to realize is that the cause-effect relationship between a bitter person not forgiving and the heart being subsequently afflicted with increased anger and bitterness, is not rooted in an isolated choice to not forgive. Rather it is rooted in a toxic state of being that makes forgiveness (among other healthy options) effectively an *impossibility*. Thus, the singular cause-effect relationship that is being observed is merely one in a multitude of destructive suffering that afflicts anyone suffering from untreated toxic anger and bitterness.

There are at least two significant differences between a bitter person not forgiving, and an emotionally healthy person not forgiving. First, and most profoundly, a bitter person doesn't have the emotional resources that make forgiveness a realistic option. However, the emotionally healthy person has the emotional resources to forgive, but for whatever reason (which is their God-given right), they choose not to. Second, for the bitter person, the decision to not forgive leads to increased bitterness and degenerate mental and emotional health. However, for the emotionally healthy person, the decision to not forgive leads to no negative effect on their mental and emotional health—or it actually *improves* it.

Raw Anger and Bitterness

Before discussing the real cause of toxic anger and bitterness, it is important to acknowledge the existence of *raw* anger and bitterness, as the latter can exhibit some identical traits to toxic anger and bitterness.

In the context of this book, I define *raw anger and bitterness* as the initial deeply felt feelings of rage that are incited as a natural result of the survivor fully processing for the first time the extent of harm and wrongdoing they suffered from the abuser or aggressor. This rawness of feeling can occur immediately following the abuse or aggression, or it can be delayed for any length of time, even years following the trauma. For survivors of child abuse, a delayed reaction is normal, as the natural state of children is to assume that their parents are good, safe, and generally well-meaning.

What raw anger and bitterness has in common with toxic anger and bitterness is that it generally renders true forgiveness effectively an impossibility while the survivor is in that state. Due to the visceral feelings of pain and resentment, considering forgiveness while the rage is raw is not entirely realistic for most people. This is even more so the case if the survivor imagines (or hopes) that forgiving will miraculously result in full emotional healing.

The mind, heart, and spirit need to first process and comprehend what actually happened before moving on to decide how to deal with the abuser or wrongdoer. If any decision to forgive is made during the period of raw anger and bitterness, it will likely be rooted in (and mixed with) toxic shame or guilt, particularly for those who have been raised or taught to consistently put themselves last. This is because the initial processing stage often induces a feeling of self-loathing and merciless self-blame, especially for those who were harmed or abused by someone who provided for them or whom they believe still love and care for them. Consequently, rushing to forgive the abuser is the survivor's way of making up for the "sin" of feeling anger or bitterness toward a "good" or "sincere" person. However, for those suffering from raw anger and bitterness, the inability to forgive is temporary and circumstantial, not permanent or character-based.

Another trait that raw anger and bitterness shares with toxic anger and bitterness is the potential for increased anger and bitterness if the anger and bitterness are not handled healthily. In raw anger and bitterness, a healthy response is to allow its expression in ways that don't cause harm to the self or others. In contrast, in toxic anger and bitterness, there is no expression of rage that does not cause harm to the self or others.

In both cases, getting to the root of the anger and bitterness is crucial. In raw anger and bitterness, the root is the emotional wounding sustained from (thus far) unaddressed trauma. In toxic anger and bitterness, the root may *include* unaddressed trauma, but its principle source is much deeper.

The Root of Toxic Anger and Bitterness

Toxic anger and bitterness is rooted in a person's heart and spirit processing trauma or perceived harm in self-destructive way. This self-destructive processing is often due to a person's frustration with how things should have been or should have turned out for them. Beneath this toxic frustration is a contradictory mental image of how the world *should* work for them on the one side, and how the world *did* work for them on the other side. In this, they feel cheated from the life they deserve, as they believe things should have worked out in a specific manner that has thus far eluded them. Therefore, this person is unable or unwilling to accept what happened and move on. Thus, in essence the person is unhealthily fixated on the past in the present, making true healing an impossibility, as healing requires living in the present despite the past.

Ironically, another root of toxic anger and bitterness is forgiveness as practiced as a result of forced forgiveness. In one scenario, the person lives with repressed anger that is never addressed healthily, so the anger ferments into toxic anger and bitterness that even the person herself is not fully conscious of. As the fermented anger continues to take over the person's life, the person continues to suppress anger, as she is still committed to only the "positive" emotions that forgiveness culture says are the only option for "good people." In needing to continuously see herself as good, the person becomes pathologically passive aggressive while viewing all her behavior as sincere and motivated by good intentions, even as she continuously harms others.

In another scenario, a victim of forced forgiveness realizes after some time that he has been manipulated in the name of forgiving abusers and wrongdoers. Having been taught that all expression of anger, hurt, or frustration is wrong, sinful, or indicative of bad character, he repressed all anger in sincere efforts to be a "good person." Because forced forgiveness culture teaches that positive emotions are for "good people" and negative emotions are for "bad people," he tried desperately to be a good person by identifying solely with positive feelings such as happiness, optimism, kindness, and forgiveness.

However, because human nature dictates that all repressed anger will ultimately implode, when it does, the person realizes the faulty nature of forgiveness (as he was taught it) and thus rejects the concept entirely, as well as all of the "fake positivity" it entails. Furthermore, as the person sustains repeated mental, emotional, and physical problems as a result of for years adhering to the dysfunctional culture of forced forgiveness, he feels more and more cheated and angry at being robbed of a fulfilling life.

As he continuously processes the betrayal by all the people, environments, and belief systems that taught forced forgiveness and behavior control and continuously favored oppressors and abusers, he refuses to be "duped" again. Thus, he commits himself to a life of self-protection through allowing not a single person, environment, or belief system to harm, trick, or manipulate him again.

For people suffering from this, it is not the peddling of forgiveness that will encourage them to heal their toxic anger and bitterness, but the validation of their anger and bitterness, as well as permission to *not* forgive. Additionally, they need to re-learn what it means to be a positive, good, well-rounded person, which includes both acknowledgment of hurts and healthy expression of anger. Furthermore, all of this effective rewiring of the mind and heart needs to happen in an environment free of blame, false positivity, or emotional manipulation aimed at convincing them that they must or should forgive.

In spiritual terms, regardless of its worldly root and how it manifests in one's life, toxic anger and bitterness is generally due to a distrust of or dissatisfaction with God. This can manifest as openly expressed frustration or anger with God, or it can manifest as repressed frustration or anger with God, which the person is unaware of, is unwilling to admit, or is terrified to address. A person who suffers from toxic anger and bitterness often does not trust God and thus lives life trusting only his or her own abilities and perceptions in ensuring safety and self-protection.

If the toxic anger and bitterness was incited by forced forgiveness culture in the context of religion, the person will likely reject God and religion altogether due to imagining that "organized religion" is merely a tool used by oppressors and abusers to control or harm others. The person will consistently refer to God and the unseen spiritual world of Paradise and Hellfire as mythology and fantasy, and thus insist that all avenging of wrongs must be done on earth (because it is the only reality).

Spiritually, people come out of toxic anger and bitterness in one of two ways: relearning the meaning of God and faith in the proper way, sans forced forgiveness and other dysfunctional manmade behavior-control systems often taught under the umbrella of religion; or ascribing to or creating a new manmade religion that embraces spirituality but rejects the labels "God" and/or "religion." This relabeling of spiritual reality allows them to benefit from the inherent spiritual nature (*fitrah*) that God created within all humans while ostensibly freeing themselves from the "shackles" of formal belief in God and the teachings of organized religion.

However, in only the former case is the person truly free from toxic anger and bitterness, as the latter case just redirects the person's anger and bitterness toward the labels "God" and "religion," even as he or she appears emotionally healthy otherwise.

8
Distinguishing Faith From Forgiveness

"We don't have to forgive unacceptable acts upon us, and nor does that make us unhealthy or 'bad.' Maybe it makes us smart, self-loving and a person of value."
—Sherrie Campbell, PhD, "The 5 Faults With Forgiveness"

◆

As I came to understand the source of my own repressed anger, I began a healing journey that challenged nearly everything I was taught about my faith as it related to my obligation to others. In uncovering the reasons behind my urge to end my life, my unexpected emotional outbursts (in anger and tears), and my failing health, I realized that my very life—physically, mentally, and spiritually—depended on the path I took toward emotional healing. In this, I became intensely aware of the nature of the spirit-soul's connection to the heart, mind, and body. In the book <u>Reverencing the Wombs That Broke You</u>, I expound upon the details of this spirit-soul and heart-mind-body connection and its relation to every person's emotional wounding and suffering.

As I came to understand the nuances involved in my own emotional wounding and suffering, I was able to move forward on a clear path to emotional healing. Through my increased awareness, I learned of the deep wounding that my spirit had sustained, and why this wounding resulted in my suicidality, depression, and physical ailments. Because the spirit-soul essence is inextricably connected to the heart, mind, and body, my emotional suffering negatively affected my spiritual practice and how I understood my faith.

In seeking healing, I made the decision to purge from my life, as far as I was reasonably able, all toxic relationships and environments, no matter how much I was connected to them through unhealthy guilt and obligation. In my book <u>*I Almost Left*</u>

Islam: How I Reclaimed My Faith, I reflect on this decision:

> As I struggled to regain my *emaan*, I realized that I had become a different person, someone I didn't recognize completely. Some of this was good, some of this was problematic, but I think most of it was just the natural progression of moving forward with life and uncovering who I really was deep inside…
>
> I became more aware of the toxic relationships in my life, and I made a conscious decision to engage in self-care and prioritize my soul above all else, even people I loved. Consequently, I removed myself from toxic relationships, business projects, and environments that were unhealthy for my mental, emotional, and spiritual health.
>
> By far, after connecting to Allah and holding on to my *emaan* independent of religious sects and elitism, making the choice to remove toxic people and environments from my life was the best decision I have ever made. As cliché as it sounds, this decision introduced me to a level of internal peace and happiness that I didn't even know existed in this worldly life. No, I do not mean that all my problems and sadness miraculously disappeared. I mean that as I faced the natural trials, pain, and struggles that were inevitable in life, I experienced for the first time a level of peace, happiness, and joy that only comes from engaging in genuine self-care and soul-preservation—minus the toxicity (2017).

During my healing journey, the topic of forgiveness continually came up in both religious and mental health contexts. As I found myself increasingly triggered by this topic, I began to explore the emotional trauma beneath this wounding. As I alluded to earlier, I came to understand that part of this was due to the aspect of forced forgiveness culture that demands passivity and apathy in response to modern day anti-Black racism. I was further able to identify emotional wounding connected to how I was taught to continuously serve, please, and obey others to the detriment of myself.

Having been taught that this servitude and self-sacrifice was a commandment of God—irrespective of whether or not it led to self-harm or poor self-care—I became frustrated with the "deny yourself to please others" ideology underlying forced forgiveness. Nothing in these discussions was about me and my emotional needs, and everything was about absolving oppressors and wrongdoers of fault and accountability for their behavior. Of course, forced forgiveness peddlers *claimed* that the shifting of focus to absolving oppressors and abusers would somehow cure me. But deep down, I knew this was not only untrue, but also that this belief was a form of emotional harm itself.

But doesn't your religion teach you to sacrifice for others? I would berate myself. *Doesn't God say you should forgive others?* Then I would feel horrible about myself, and the cycle of depression and feeling unworthy of being alive would threaten to suffocate me again. It was through weathering this internal spiritual and emotional battle that I came to understand the problem with failing to distinguish matters of faith from options of forgiveness and self-sacrifice.

Oprah's Healing and Forced Forgiveness

Undoubtedly, one of the most influential American personalities on matters of self-awareness, personal improvement, and emotional healing is Oprah Winfrey. The widespread positive influence of her inspirational nature and serene charisma are arguably unparalleled in television history. The positive effect that she has on others is usually reserved for in-person relationships, whether in therapy or friendships. In sharing her own healing journey following abuse and loss, Oprah has awakened in the American consciousness the need to embrace love and forgiveness as a way of life. As such, her story has effectively become one of the most powerful real-life proofs that forced forgiveness is a *good* thing.

In defining *forgiveness*, Oprah refers to one man's definition that resonated most with her when he was a guest on her show: "It really means letting go of the past we thought we wanted." In reflecting on this, Oprah says in an episode from *Oprah's Lifeclass*, "That was a *transcendent* moment for me — bigger, even, than an *aha* [moment]. He said forgiveness is giving up the hope that the past could be any different."

Oprah goes on to say, "It took me to the next level of being a better person." She then offers viewers advice for their own lives:

"I don't hold grudges for anything or any situation — and neither should you. [Forgiveness] is letting go so that the past does not hold you prisoner" (HuffingtonPost.com, March 2013).

When looking at Oprah's definition of forgiveness, it is undeniable that believing with all your heart that the past could not be any different is a crucial part of healing. However, the problem with this definition is that it has absolutely nothing at all to do with forgiveness.

Faith, Forgiveness, and Healing

In Islamic tradition, there are six pillars of *emaan*, which can be translated as sincere faith or authentic spirituality. The first pillar is having sincere faith or belief in Allah (the Arabic term for God or the One who has sole right to worship), and the last pillar is having sincere faith in the *qadr*. It is this last pillar of faith that encompasses Oprah's definition of forgiveness.

In simple terms, *qadr* can be translated as divine decree or predestination. It refers to the fact that everything that occurs in life unfolds exactly according to what has already been written and decreed by God. However, *qadr* does not negate human choice or accountability; it includes it. Nevertheless, once an event has passed, it is quintessential to *emaan* itself to fully accept with a humble, sincere heart that things could not have turned out differently. Thus, it is upon the one endowed with true and sincere spirituality to move forward in acceptance of *qadr* and glean the necessary life lessons from that experience.

Interestingly, one of the most famous prophetic narrations regarding the six pillars of faith mentions these words following the necessity to believe in the *qadr*: "both the good and evil thereof." In other words, it is a fundamental part of *emaan* to humbly accept the natural duality of human life: pleasure and pain; happiness and sadness; health and sickness; and so on. Thus, for those already endowed with authentic spirituality, Oprah's transcendent, "bigger than an *aha*" moment is merely a basic, rudimentary part of living life with a heart full of faith. Forgiveness, however, is another matter entirely.

9

Success and Sincerity in Forced Forgiveness

"Dear tongue, be still. You know not how your utterances will harm the spirits of those who do not live in this body."
—from the journal of Umm Zakiyyah

◆

Though Oprah's definition of *forgiveness* is not actually forgiveness, this does not mean that her (or anyone else's) emotional healing is incomplete, faulty, or disingenuous. Nor does it mean that Oprah has not *also* engaged in forgiveness in addition to engaging in acceptance. It is fully possible (and I would imagine it is quite likely) that Oprah's acceptance of the past has indeed also meant forgiveness for her. Thus, what is important here is not any alleged faultiness in Oprah's personal experience, but the inherent faultiness in seeking to make her personal truth *our* personal truth.

While there are some for whom Oprah's journey of "forgiveness" (i.e. acceptance that includes forgiveness) fully resonates, this does not make the culture of forced forgiveness any less dysfunctional or harmful in itself. Just as each human has a genetic makeup and physiological sensitivities unique to him or her, so it is with emotional and spiritual needs and sensitivities for each individual. There are certainly foundational emotional and spiritual truths that apply to all human beings, but the teachings of forced forgiveness culture are not among them.

Whenever we tap into narcissism instead of authentic spirituality to guide others on their healing journeys, we inevitably fall into subtle abuse through manipulation and harm, even when we have the best of intentions and sincerest of hearts. For this reason, nearly all spiritual traditions emphasize focusing on the self and respecting the sanctity of others' lives, families, and properties. These faith traditions have a multitude of proverbs and principles that guide how we are to use our tongues and limbs in this world, as well as our hearts and minds, for this noble purpose.

In the context of emotional healing, we would do well to reflect on the fact that respecting the sacredness of someone else's life, family, and property is not limited to the physical realm of existence. The bodily home that encloses the human spirit-soul is no more our right to violate than the physical home that encloses others' intimate life, family, and personal property. While our personal experiences and successes might be fully authentic for our lives (and those with similar realities), the authenticity and rightness of our personal paths to healing do not equal them being authentic and right for others' paths to healing.

Harms of Manmade Spirituality

Due to the widespread suffering of humanity as a result of humans altering divine concepts for their own selfish purposes then attributing their manmade additions and subtractions to God, most of us have very strong (and sometimes emotionally charged) opinions against "the faithful" forcing their religious practices on others. In this, we do not even care whether or not the religious person is sincere and wants "good" for us (according to their subjective definition of the term). We deem their views oppressive, backward, evil, and extreme; and understandably so. However, hypocritically, many self-proclaimed spiritual people—many of whom follow (or claim to *be*) gurus and experts on emotional healing—fail to realize when they are guilty of the same mentality under the umbrella of forced forgiveness.

No oppressive culture or society was able to achieve widespread harm except that there were ostensibly good and empowering ideas and beliefs spread beforehand. In the beginning stages, these concepts appear necessary for whatever short-term goal is before society, and in their initial, pure forms, these ideas might in fact *be* necessary. However, as time goes on, these "good" ideas become the "only" ideas in addressing an issue. As a result, the society evolves from an environment of encouraging good to an oppressive system *forcing* "good."

I don't mention this socio-political reality to suggest that forced forgiveness culture will lead to bloody wars, persecution of the innocent, or any form of "religious" genocide. I mention this reality for the same reason that I mentioned the obligation of respecting others' property above. The obligation to respect human life is not only physical. It is also emotional and spiritual.

Just as a seemingly good political concept like democracy is true democracy only insomuch as it is not violently forced upon a non-democratic nation, a beneficial healing concept like forgiveness is true forgiveness only insomuch as it is not forced upon an unwilling survivor. In the political realm, democracy ceases to be beneficial if the people don't choose it. In the spiritual and emotional realm, forgiveness ceases to be healing if the survivor doesn't choose it.

Similarly, just as manmade concepts introduced into organized religion ultimately cause harm to others, manmade concepts introduced into authentic spirituality and emotional healing also cause harm to others. For this reason, it is important for humans, no matter how well-meaning, to frame their emotional healing stories as personal testimonies that others might find helpful, not as licenses to accuse survivors of having angry, bitter, and corrupt hearts if someone's healing journey doesn't mirror theirs.

A Culture of Manipulation and Harm

In the absence of understanding authentic spirituality, advocates of forced forgiveness have created a culture of subtle abuse despite their inspirational stories and good intentions. As is well-known in cases of blatant abuse, the lack of conscious intent to abuse (by the abuser) does not preclude the very real experience of abuse (for the one suffering it).

Nevertheless, it is important to note that unintentionally participating in a culture of abuse does not necessarily make someone an abuser per se, just as doing something bad does not necessarily make someone a bad person per se. No one is perfect, and it is likely that we have all participated in cultures of harm at some point in our lives, even if only unwittingly. For this reason, I refer to the abuse in forced forgiveness culture as being *subtle* in its essence (though no less harmful).

While there are certainly advocates of forced forgiveness that use blatant emotional manipulation and obvious passive aggressiveness to convince others to forgive, it is my belief that the vast majority of proponents of forced forgiveness are sincere, well-meaning people who genuinely want to share their tools of happiness with the world.

True Forgiveness

Regarding the heart, there is only one condition of true forgiveness: sincerity. In Islamic tradition, sincerity is *ikhlaas*, and in the context of forgiveness, it means that one's decision is voluntary and non-coerced, and that it is rooted in one's pure belief in God and the desire to earn His divine love, favor, or forgiveness. As such, it is possible that a person voluntarily chooses to forgive even as they are fully aware that their full emotional healing may elude them for some time.

10
The Gift of Not Forgiving

"In acceptance the healing is about you. In forgiveness the healing is about the perpetrator."
—Sherrie Campbell, PhD, "The 5 Faults With Forgiveness"

◆

"Are you really saying that you are so arrogant that you would not forgive your Muslim brother if he asks you to?" This question was posed to me in the midst of a discussion following the racist statements made by a renowned White American Muslim scholar. In a speech to a predominately non-Black audience at an annual Islamic conference, this White American imam and convert to Islam trivialized the reality of police brutality and murder of Black people, saying that white people had it worse. The scholar then stated that racism was not the biggest problem facing Black people in America; it was the breakdown of the Black family.

In other words, even though racism negatively affected Black people more than any other group, and even though family problems negatively affected *every* human group, the pathology and brokenness of the Black family was so bad that widespread oppression itself paled in comparison. And in keeping with the dysfunctional culture of forced forgiveness, the focus of discussions thereafter was less on addressing the problematic statements themselves, but on harassing the people who felt anger and hurt at his words. Continuously, we were reminded of how good of a person this imam was and that it was a sin to focus on this "one mistake."

It is indeed ironic that for all the compassion and understanding that adherents of forced forgiveness show to people guilty of hurting others, this compassion and understanding miraculously disappears when they are dealing with those wounded by hurtful words or behavior itself. It is as if, subconsciously, they believe that wrongdoers are generally good and victims are generally evil. Thus, it is only the former who deserve swift and unconditional compassion, excuses, and forgiveness; while the latter deserve swift and unconditional harassment, emotional manipulation, and slanderous statements about their mental and spiritual state.

It continuously astounds me how the excuses and claims of inherent goodness routinely abound for aggressors, even with no evidence of contrition or changed behavior; and the insults and claims of inherent corruption and bitterness routinely abound for sufferers, even with clear evidence of their attempt to cope and heal despite the hurtful or emotionally traumatic situation. This phenomenon alone speaks volumes about the subtle abuse and toxicity inherent in forced forgiveness culture.

Sometimes forgiveness peddlers defend this hypocrisy by claiming that the hurtful incident (like the one involving the White American scholar) was really just a matter of one person's subjective perspective on a controversial issue, not evidence of any clear wrongdoing. However, they fail to have a clear answer as to why then is it only those who feel hurt who are labeled corrupt and sinful. Why aren't these people's statements of disagreement viewed as a "legitimate subjective perspective" on a controversial issue—instead of as evidence of some inherent evil within them? Furthermore, why don't forgiveness peddlers stand up to defend these people's goodness with as much fervor as they do the ones who inflict the harm (even if unintentionally)?

Furthermore, if having only positive, good feelings toward everyone is the only acceptable way to live life, why then are so many forgiveness peddlers consistently negative, passive aggressive, and insulting toward those who have chosen to not forgive? Why do they brag so much about forgiving even those who have neither asked for forgiveness nor shown any remorse, yet they appear utterly incapable of avoiding cruelty and character assassination of those who are merely trying to heal in peace without harming anyone?

Or perhaps they imagine that speaking softly and smiling while showing cruelty and insulting "unforgiving" survivors means they have not deviated from their "I forgive everyone" ideology of life? If so, why are the cruelty and insults directed at only survivors, and not abusers? Meanwhile, if survivors were to use the *same* negative and cruel language in describing their abusers, forgiveness peddlers would accuse *them* of being angry, bitter, and unforgiving—even if the survivor spoke in the same soft voice and wore the same sincere smile as the forgiveness peddler.

Why the disconnect and double standard? Why are proponents of forced forgiveness so blind to their own negativity and cruelty in speaking to and about those they imagine haven't forgiven? I realize that not *all* adherents to forced forgiveness openly engage in cruelty and insults toward "unforgiving" survivors. But nearly all hold the same insulting views about not forgiving, whether they vocalize this negative judgment or not.

The Gift of Self-Care

People often say that forgiveness is a gift you give yourself more than it is a gift you give the other person. While this is true depending on one's definition, understanding, and practice of forgiveness; you still cannot give a gift from resources you do not have. And there are times when *not* giving a gift is wiser and healthier for you (and the other person) than giving it. Yes, generally speaking, forgiveness and gift giving are beautiful things, and it is undeniable that both soften the heart and spread love amongst people. However, this is true only when gifts are given from a place of sincerity and do not deplete one's basic resources. The same is true for forgiveness.

Nearly every culture has the tradition of gift giving as a ritual of spreading love, happiness, and joy amongst themselves and others. And nearly everyone relishes in the joy of giving and receiving gifts. However, anyone who has had the unfortunate experience of being criticized, insulted, or slandered due to giving someone a gift they didn't like or due to not giving someone a gift at all knows the harmful side of gift-giving when it devolves into *forced* gift-giving practices.

On this topic, I once read a humorous statement that made me burst into laughter. I can't remember who said it and in what context. Perhaps it was a comedian. But I recall the man saying that he had become so broke and distressed due to the pressures of

America's forced gift-giving culture that he changes religions once a year. From November through January, he is a Muslim convert. From February through October, he returns to being Christian. That way, whenever someone starts hinting at any gifts they want, he can just tell them he doesn't celebrate Christmas. Once the holiday season winds down, he goes back to his religion.

Obviously, forced gift giving is not unique to Christian culture. In many predominately Muslim cultures, a similar mindset surrounds not only Eid but also visits to one's home country if one is a citizen in the West. I myself have personally witnessed the extreme distress of Muslims worrying that they would unable to give their friends and relatives what was expected during the visit. I have also heard of humorous ruses devised to avoid the conundrum altogether.

I mention this to say that the healing nature of forgiveness and spreading of love due to gift giving are general rules, not inflexible, hard and fast ones that have no exceptions. Earlier, I discussed the important distinction between being an unforgiving person and a person choosing not to forgive. A similar distinction exists between being a stingy person and a person choosing not to give a gift. A person can be generally generous and giving yet decide to not give a gift in certain circumstances. This decision could be due to a lack of financial resources or even due to wishing to abate others' manipulation or feelings of entitlement. Making the isolated decision to not forgive is no different.

However, the gift we always owe ourselves is self-care, and the gift we owe others is supporting their self-care. Whenever we ascribe to forced gift giving, whether through physical gifts or spiritual ones like forgiveness, we run the risk of denying ourselves the gift of self care. Likewise, when we tell others they must ascribe to forced gift giving, we are not only *not* supporting their self-care, we are also causing them harm—even if we genuinely have their best interests at heart.

When Forgiving Depletes Emotional Resources

Just as spending more money than we have depletes our financial resources and puts us in literal debt and potential bankruptcy, spending more emotional resources than we have puts us in emotional debt and crisis of the spirit. This crisis of the spirit, which can be viewed as a sort of emotional bankruptcy, then begins to deplete the emotional, mental, and even physical resources we need for our own basic survival. Sometimes this state leads to nervous breakdowns, anxiety attacks, depression, and spiritual crisis.

It is certainly possible that making the choice to forgive can itself restore some of those emotional and spiritual resources. However, this is only possible if continuous, obligatory "forgiveness" is not what depleted the resources in the first place. Furthermore, this restoration is only possible if the person's heart truly has the emotional resources to sincerely forgive at that time. If our emotional wounding has affected our spirituality such that we haven't yet fully accepted the *qadr* of what happened, then we should first address this deep spiritual wounding before we seek to rejuvenate a spirit that is not even whole.

For those who are emotionally wounded due to continuously being taken advantage of by others and then forced to forgive and give, give, give, their spiritual and emotional rejuvenation will likely come from analyzing what happened to them and making the conscious decision to *not* forgive. This choice can then become empowering in bolstering self-care and drawing limits on what they will and will not accept in life.

If later down the road, they decide to forgive, this is fine. However, at the moment of feeling used and abused, feeling anger and blame toward the wrongdoer is healthiest—so long as this feeling does not involve harming the self or others, or transgressing the bounds of healthy spirituality. Of course, a person can feel anger and blame *and* forgive, but this is not always realistic or healthiest for a person whose entire emotional trauma is rooted in being denied the right to *not* forgive.

11
Self Deception in Forgiveness Culture

"We can fool ourselves, but we cannot fool God."
—unknown

◆

When I found myself fighting thoughts of suicide, I realized that emotional health was not as simple as freeing my heart from anger and resentment toward others, or as simple as choosing to forgive the ones who wronged me or even as simple as humbly and sincerely accepting divine *qadr*. I realized that there was a level of dignity and self-respect, as well as emotional wellbeing and healthy spirituality, involved in deliberately identifying with negative emotions and making the "not so nice" choice to refuse to be mistreated and abused.

As a direct result of this newfound level of emotional health, I made the decision to restore *not* forgiving as a healthy, sometimes necessary personal choice in life. Though I'd never consciously stopped thinking of forgiveness as a personal choice, I came to realize that on many unconscious levels, I myself ascribed to forced forgiveness culture—and routinely guilted myself into forgiving before I'd even processed or admitted what had happened to me. Also, I came to realize that I had done my own share of forgiveness peddling to others before I was tested with spiritual crisis and then understood the inherent harm in this.

In seeking to overcome the emotional wounding of forced forgiveness, I viewed self-care as not only a gift I owed myself, but as also a spiritual obligation to my spirit-soul essence that defined *me*. I further viewed self-care as a gift I owed the bodily home that enclosed my spirit-soul on earth. Thus, if safeguarding my soul meant forgiving someone, then I would forgive, and if safeguarding my soul meant not forgiving someone, then I wouldn't forgive. However, as a general rule, my default soul-preservation remained in choosing forgiveness.

In reflecting on my newfound level of emotional healing, I could say that my heart no longer harbors any anger or blame toward anyone. I could say that I no longer hold grudges. I could even say that I am completely emotionally healed and spiritually pure. But I won't. If there is one lesson I learned throughout my healing journey, it is this: There will always be parts of ourselves that are unknown to us and thus exist beyond our level of perception and comprehension. And the wise person remains silent regarding the unseen.

No matter how spiritually aware we are and no matter how attuned we are to the energy and vibrations of our spirit-soul existence, as long as we are alive, we are still learning and we are still growing. Thus, we forever remain students of the unseen realities of our soul. Moreover, the spirit-soul world is such a mysterious and powerful one that we can perceive one thing about it while our spiritual reality is entirely different.

Also, because this spirit-soul world is so intricately connected to *qadr*—the life and trials that are decreed for us on earth—we can find ourselves at peace with what feels like a healthy spiritual existence but is in fact merely our spirit submitting to a trial of the soul instead of an elevation of it. As a general rule, spiritual elevation is found in the internal battle of soul, not in its complete stillness or in a sustainable static state. This is because complete spiritual tranquility is reserved for the afterlife, as this worldly life is defined by continuous trials—until the spirit-soul is removed from its earthly shell.

For this reason, God repeatedly advises us to look at the signs within us and around us to guide our spiritual journeys in life. Feelings and perceptions are important parts of these signs, but they are not the full essence of them. Thus, we can conceivably feel and perceive that we are connecting to our "authentic self," yet we are merely submitting to the path that leads to our "authentic" destination in the Hereafter. This destination could be eternal bliss, or it could be eternal torment. Both represent a level of authenticity unique to our individual existence on earth.

Therefore, it is crucial that we differentiate the authenticity of our *qadr* (our unique life path) from the authenticity of our *fitrah* (natural, uncorrupted spirituality). Our ultimate spiritual success in life lies in uniting them. I reflect on this phenomenon in my journal:

> When discussing our "authentic self," there are two possibilities: the authentic self of our *fitrah* (perfect nature) and the authentic self of our *qadr* (ultimate fate). Our *fitrah* is based on our natural propensity toward treading a path of obedience to Allah, and our *qadr* is based on treading a path toward our ultimate fate in the Hereafter. Oftentimes, when people talk about living a life that reflects their "authentic self", they do not differentiate between these two. Naturally, although we know (at least in the general sense) what obeying Allah looks like, we cannot possibly know what our fate in the Hereafter looks like. Thus, if we find ourselves being propelled toward disobeying Allah (which suggests a negative fate in the Hereafter), we need to, as the saying goes, "fight *qadr* with *qadr*." In other words, we need to use our *fitrah* to constantly fight the possibility of a terrible fate in the Hereafter, no matter how authentic disobeying Allah feels to us in this life.

In reflecting on this profound reality, I reflect on this verse of the Qur'an: "…So ascribe not purity to yourselves. He (Allah) knows best who fears Allah and keeps his duty to Him" (*An-Najm*, 53:32). This verse teaches us at least two things about our spirit-soul existence: One, authentic spirituality is rooted in humbly striving for goodness, not in claiming it for oneself. Two, the very definition of goodness is reflected in a life of obedience to God (or Allah in Arabic).

Therefore, a person who is truly experiencing spiritual purity may speak about her perceptions regarding what is or is not in her heart, but she does not make firm declarations about its purity. For example, a spiritually intelligent person would say, "I perceive no ill feelings in my heart toward anyone" as opposed to "I have no ill feelings in my heart toward anyone."

Regarding our praising of others, Islamic tradition narrates this advice from Prophet Muhammad (peace be upon him): "If one of you is to definitely praise his brother, then let him say: 'I deem such and such [to be like that] and I do not praise anyone above Allah, [as] Allah is his Reckoner'— if he believes that he is like that" (Bukhari and Muslim).

In other words, authentic spirituality guards us against the pitfalls of unperceived narcissism, arrogance, and self-deception, all of which manifest in both covert and overt ways. When these are covert, we feel like we are good, sincere people, even as we are falling into spiritual self-deception. When these are overt, we don't even care whether or not we are good, sincere people, as authentic spirituality is not even our concern. Undoubtedly, the former is much more common in humanity than the latter, as most humans want to at least believe they are good people, even if they are not.

However, both forms of spiritual misguidance (covert and overt) manifest as external signs in our speech or behavior, which are spiritual alerts that something is amiss in our hearts and souls. The more spiritually healthy we are, the more guilt, dislike, and regret we feel when our speech or behavior is incongruent with what God requires of us on earth. The more spiritually misguided we are, the more disobeying God feels "authentic" and "natural" to us. Those suffering the worst form of spiritual misguidance begin to not only see good as evil and evil as good; but they also create (or follow) alternate spiritual paths and call people away from authentic spirituality.

The Problem with Success Stories of Forgiveness

Simply put, the problem with success stories regarding others' experience with forgiveness, specifically when they include testimonies of what is happening in their hearts, is that we are hearing about only their perceptions and feelings, not their true spiritual realities. Given the nature of denial and repressed anger, especially in the context of forced forgiveness (which produces both), it is impossible to know whether or not a person is truly emotionally healed or merely at the stage of unawareness preceding emotional implosion.

Nevertheless, when we understand forgiveness properly (i.e. as defined by authentic spirituality), someone's internal spiritual or emotional reality is completely irrelevant to their success with forgiveness. As discussed earlier, the only condition of true forgiveness is sincerity, which is termed *ikhlaas* in Arabic. Thus, if a person sincerely intends to forgive—even if he has not fully emotionally healed (or even if he is unaware of denial and repressed anger beneath the surface)—God accepts this sincerity and rewards him immensely for the selfless choice.

If the person later finds repressed anger surfacing, God will bestow His mercy upon the person due to his sincerity, and guide him through the painful process of healthily releasing anger. However, this emotional difficulty in no way negates the sincerity of his earlier forgiveness, even if it was technically premature according to the worldly definition of forgiveness.

In a famous hadith, Prophet Muhammad (peace be upon him) said, "Actions are by intention, and everyone shall get what he intended" (Bukhari and Muslim). Therefore, if any person forgives someone who wronged him while sincerely hoping God will reward him for that choice, then God will reward him for that choice—even if the person does not yet fully comprehend what true emotional healing requires.

12

But Doesn't God Love Forgiveness?

"Forgiveness can be sweet and healing; that's no lie. But please, before counseling forgiveness, take heed of the power and diversity of injuries as well as the nature of the person or group you are counseling. If we counsel forgiveness as a general practice, we turn a blind eye to so many—a blind eye that may put salt on wounds or add a layer of shame for those whom forgiveness is not the next step."
—David Bedrick, "6 Reasons Not to Forgive, Not Yet"

◆

But why not *forgive?* so the question goes. *Doesn't God love forgiveness? If your heart is truly full of faith, then wouldn't you naturally forgive?* The answer to this lies in, again, differentiating faith from forgiveness and understanding that true spirituality necessitates embracing the full definition of faith and human goodness, not only those parts that make us feel "warm and fuzzy" inside.

Thus, I would ask the questioner this: *Why do* you *not embrace all of God's teachings about addressing wrongdoing? Why is it only forgiveness you accept? Do you imagine you know better than God? And since you are posing this question to someone else, why do* you *go against God's instructions to stay away from blaming the innocent?*

Of course, I ask these questions only to those who are posing their questions as challenges, criticisms, and emotional manipulation, as opposed to as sincere curiosity for the purpose of understanding the topic better. The reason these questions are more relevant than the emotionally manipulative ones aimed at guilting survivors is that in the answer to the above questions is the answer to theirs: God obligates us to focus on ourselves.

If survivors of abuse and wrongdoing are focusing on what they believe is best for them while not wronging anyone in the process, why can't we do the same ourselves? At best, the answers to our questions are none of our business, and at worst, we are falling into sin by disobeying God and harming innocent people. If we are counselors, life coaches, or mental health professionals trying to help a client, we need to take a step back and do a little more study of this topic before we cause more harm than help.

Guilting Victims Is Disobeying God

It is undeniable that God loves forgiveness. It is also undeniable that God views forgiveness as exponentially more superior than blame, punishment, and retaliation. Personally, I highly doubt that there is in existence a single survivor, even one trapped in toxic anger and bitterness, who would deny this fact. So the question here isn't really about God loving forgiveness. Rather, the question is about whether or not *we*—the judgmental outsiders (even if we happen to be survivors)—accept that God also loves justice.

The question is also about whether or not we sincerely accept that God supports *whatever* decision victims of wrongdoing make in addressing what happened to them, so long as they don't violate anyone's rights in the process.

In forced forgiveness culture, the answer is no to both of these questions: No, we don't accept that God loves justice, and no, we don't accept that God supports victims' right to choice. Yes, many of us give lip service to acknowledging this. But the words are like a dismissive wave of the hand before we get right back to guilting survivors of abuse into doing what *we* say they must, God's teachings be damned.

Ironically, in this forced forgiveness approach, it is we ourselves who are in danger of falling into sin and wrongdoing. And this danger is much more imminent than the hypothetical possibility of a survivor's heart being filled with anger and bitterness if they don't forgive. However, we are too busy imagining that we know better than everyone else, God included, to even perceive the looming harm hanging over our own hearts and souls.

In Islamic tradition, there are many places in the Qur'an in which God describes the traits of sincere believers. In one part, He prefaces this description with a reminder of the nature of the things humans enjoy in this worldly life. He says what has been translated to mean:

> "So whatever you have been given is but a passing enjoyment for this worldly life, but that which is with Allah (i.e. Paradise) is better and more lasting for those who believe and put their trust in their Lord" (*Ash-Shooraa*, 42:36).

Given that several verses that follow address both forgiveness and wrongdoing, this introduction is quite profound in that it reminds every person, regardless of circumstance, the nature of this transient world and how we should understand our experiences in it. This allows the reader to put his or her mind in the right place before even processing the traits of the sincere believers who will be in Paradise. God goes on to list several traits of these believers:

> "And those who avoid the greater sins and immoralities, and when they are angry, they forgive. And those who have responded to [the call of] their Lord and establish the *Salaah* (obligatory prayer), and who [conduct] their affairs by mutual consultation, and who spend out of what We have bestowed on them" (*Ash-Shooraa*, 42:37-38).

For those involved in forced forgiveness, they would read this description and immediately think, *See! This is what I'm talking about. God says that* true *believers forgive wrongs! So what's going on with all these angry, bitter people refusing to forgive those who wronged them?* However, in this description of those who forgive, God didn't mention wrongdoing at all. He mentioned only that they are angry. He doesn't even mention *why* they are angry. Yes, wrongdoing is certainly implied in the verse, but it is not mentioned specifically. This is no small point.

Some people might say that this wording is merely a technicality, and that I'm being nitpicky in even pointing it out. Thus, they argue that this wording has absolutely nothing to do with the fact that *everyone* should forgive, no matter what abuse, oppression, or wrongdoing they suffered. However, when we say this, what we fail to realize is that not only is the emphasis on anger quite significant; it is also *the point*, as the verses that follow make undeniably clear.

Before quoting the verses about wrongdoing, I think it is important to mention how we should understand the wording of things in the Qur'an, especially when the same topic is addressed more than once in the same context. Generally, whenever a topic is discussed more than once and in some detail, what is and is not mentioned in each context points to important traits we are to focus on in understanding them. In some cases, these important traits are found in contexts outside the Qur'an, such as in the reason for revelation and in the prophetic example. However, in this case, the important traits are mentioned quite clearly in the verses themselves.

In the above context, when forgiveness is mentioned as the immediate response, the emphasis is on the fact that the person is angry, not that he or she has been wronged. The profound wisdom in this emphasis cannot be overstated.

In our daily lives, there are many things that anger us: A friend refuses to speak to us, and we have no idea why. Someone is late picking us up to an important appointment. A business partner agreed to do something then dropped out at the last minute. A person cuts us off in traffic or quickly steals our parking space. Our husband or wife is focused more on their smartphone or career than on us. And the list goes on.

One lesson we can glean is this: When facing day-to-day things that incite anger, for the sincere believer, the default response is that of forgiveness. By praising this trait in His servants, God lets us know that our daily behavior should foster environments of peace, understanding, and empathy instead of hostility and retaliation. No one is perfect. Thus, from time to time, we'll all be insensitive, unreliable, and even flat out wrong, thereby inciting justifiable anger in others. However, as a general rule, it is in everyone's best interests to be forgiving and merciful in these circumstances. Otherwise, the world would be full of quarrelsome, vengeful people who feel justified in avenging even the slightest offense.

This is not to say that *none* of the scenarios I listed are sometimes more serious than they initially appear, or even that we *have to* forgive these scenarios every single time. I give these examples only to make the point that what is being described in the Qur'an is the fact that sincere believers—those endowed with authentic spirituality—have a *forgiving nature*. And this nature is manifested most when they are justifiably angry yet still choose to forgive.

However, when an egregious wrongdoing has occurred, the emphasis is no longer on forgiveness; it is on justice. In this case, the sincere believers are described as follows: "And those who, when an oppressive wrong is done to them, they help and defend themselves" (*Ash-Shooraa*, 42:39).

In the verse that follows, it is only after it is explained that the retribution should fit the crime that the option to forgive is mentioned:

> "The recompense for an injury is an injury equal thereto [in degree]. But if a person forgives and makes reconciliation, his reward is due from Allah. Verily, He loves not the wrongdoers" (42:40).

Interestingly, God does not stop here in discussing the rights of those who have been wronged. He goes on to let victims know that not only do they have full right to *not* forgive, but also, should they exercise that right, no one has the right to blame them in any way. He says:

> "But if any do help and defend themselves after a wrong [done] to them, against such there is no cause of blame. The blame is only against those who oppress people and insolently transgress beyond bounds through the land, defying right and justice. For such there will be a penalty grievous" (42:41-42).

Here is where seeing and understanding the original Arabic would be tremendously helpful in comprehending the powerful message being conveyed here. However, to get a glimpse of the deeper meaning, I offer this explanation: What is being translated as "there is no cause of blame" (i.e. against the victim who decides to not forgive), a more literal translation would be "there is no path, road, or means [that can be taken] against them." By using the Arabic word *sabeel*—which is translated as *cause* above but has the literal meaning of *way, path,* or *road*—God is shutting down every possible justification anyone can use to criticize, blame, or harm a victim who chooses to not forgive.

In other words, it doesn't matter whether this justification of blame, criticism, or harm is rooted in good intentions or not, if it is directed at the victim of wrongdoing, God simply does not allow it. If we do take this pathway of blame, then we are the ones who are wrong.

Even if we are simply perplexed or sincerely disappointed at their choice to not forgive, once they make their decision, we have no right to express disappointment or criticism, as this expression itself can be a *sabeel* (a pathway of blame) against them—no matter how harmless, innocent, or well meaning it appears to us.

After God makes this point crystal clear, He then effectively tells us: *If you still feel in your heart or mind any inclination to criticize, blame, or express disappointment toward anyone as a result of this circumstance [which resulted in the victim not forgiving], then shift all of your attention back to the one who started this whole problem in the first place: the abuser, wrongdoer, or oppressor:* "…The blame is only against those who oppress people and insolently transgress beyond bounds through the land, defying right and justice."

Only after God establishes beyond a shadow of a doubt the victim's full right to choice—and the prohibition of *any* form of blame or harm against them as a result of their choice—does He return to the topic of forgiveness:

> "But indeed, if any show patience and forgive, that would truly be an exercise of courageous will and resolution in the conduct of affairs" (42:43).

13

Why Forgiveness Isn't For Everyone

"Holding onto hatred and bitterness is not *the same as not forgiving. We can let go of animosity and resentment by finding peace in knowing that God will deal with a person in the Hereafter—or that they'll carry some of our sins. This allows us to live the rest of our lives with a clear, peaceful heart. So don't let anyone guilt you into forgiving if you're not ready yet, especially if you find more peace in knowing that God will deal with a person than in absolving them of accountability altogether. Yes, as a general rule, forgiveness is closest to righteousness. But God defines righteousness, and He's the One who gave the wronged the option to choose."*
—excerpt of *PAIN. From the Journal of Umm Zakiyyah*

◆

I think we've all heard the popular saying attributed to no one in particular but shared by nearly every inspirational website and social media account: *You will begin to heal when you let go of past hurts, forgive those who have wronged you, and learn to forgive yourself for your mistakes.* Unfortunately, the culture of forced forgiveness continues to spread the dysfunctional ideology that victims will be doomed to a lifetime of emotional suffering should they hold abusers accountable for their actions.

As beautiful and well-meaning as the quote may be, by telling sufferers they will "begin to heal" only after they forgive, the statement stands as a clear example of an ostensibly harmless pathway of blame being used against a victim who has exercised his or her God-given right to not forgive. What makes this pathway of blame devaluing and emotionally damaging is that survivors of abuse and wrongdoing often come across quotes like this while seeking healing from their wounds of the spirit. And these are wounds that they sustained as a result of experiencing abuse and wrongdoing—wounds which they will suffer irrespective of whether or not the abuser pays for his sins.

Even when we feel it is wisest or beneficial to encourage forgiveness (the key word here being *encourage*), we should not present forgiveness as the price that must be paid before healing takes place. Emotional trauma is deep and complex, and there is no magical choice of forgiveness that results in healing.

Complex PTSD, which includes (among other things) anxiety, emotional triggers, depression, and trust issues, is often a lifelong battle for survivors, even after they have sincerely forgiven the wrongdoers. This wounding is so nuanced that a survivor can go for a long period of time feeling completely free of symptoms, including anger and blame, and a single incident can occur that triggers these feelings all over again. Not only is this re-triggering completely out of their control, it also cannot be prevented or thwarted through forgiveness, no matter how sincere.

Thus, it is quite odd that we teach survivors that these struggles will magically disappear through the choice of forgiveness. Such a suggestion is about as logical as teaching a victim of severe physical wounding that all scars and evidence of the attack will disappear once they forgive the one who assaulted them. In this vein, deep emotional wounds aren't much different from deep bodily wounds. The only difference is that the former are felt in the spirit whereas the latter are felt in the body.

Yes, "complete recovery" is possible in both cases. However, in the context of both emotional and physical trauma, the term *complete recovery* does not mean that absolutely no scars will be visible or that absolutely no pain will ever be felt again. It simply means that you will be able live a relatively normal life after taking the necessary steps to heal as fully as possible. If the wound was in the leg, it means you will be able to walk again. If the trauma resulted in a coma, it means you will be able to think, feel, and move about again. Likewise, if the wound is in the spirit, it means you will be able to function "normally" for the most part, despite the inevitable scars and pain that may surface from time to time.

In both physical and emotional recovery, the only mindset (or condition of the spirit) that is absolutely necessary before full healing can take place is the acceptance of what happened and of the need to move forward based on what *is* instead of what *should have been*. As discussed earlier, this mindset is the sixth pillar of authentic spirituality, specifically the heart humbly accepting the unchangeable nature of *qadr* (what has already passed).

Without the acceptance of *qadr*—which has absolutely nothing to do with forgiveness—a victim of physical trauma won't likely commit to physical therapy or any other medical healing regimen; and a victim of emotional trauma won't likely commit to the regimen of therapy needed for healing. However, forgiveness is not necessary in either case of recovery. Thus, it is imperative that we cease discussing forgiveness as a condition of healing. This is even more so the case if we follow up this discussion with threats of anger and bitterness corrupting the heart. I reflect on this point in my book <u>*Pain. From the Journal of Umm Zakiyyah*</u>:

> That we discuss forgiving those who've wronged us in the same context that we discuss healing our emotional wounds suggests that we understand neither forgiveness nor healing. Forgiveness is not required before healing can take place, and though healing certainly makes forgiveness easier, healing is not required before forgiveness can take place.
>
> They are two separate things.
>
> Forgiveness simply means you seek no retribution for the wrongdoer—in this world or in the Hereafter—on account of your suffering.
>
> But healing means you are taking the necessary steps *for yourself* to tend to your wounds. This, so that you can move forward as a whole person and protect yourself from further harm.
>
> But some wrongs cut so deep that full healing is simply not possible. Nevertheless, seeking healing is a must, while granting forgiveness is a choice. And for some people, *not* forgiving fosters healing most because it puts their heart at ease knowing that God will punish the wrongdoer for what they've done.
>
> Nevertheless, forgiveness remains most praiseworthy—so long as it comes from the depths of someone's heart and not because they've been guilted into believing that they must absolve the wrongdoer before God will help them heal from something they suffered through no fault of their own (2016).

Thus, the only truly healing statement in the quote *"You will begin to heal when you let go of past hurts, forgive those who have wronged you, and learn to forgive yourself for your mistakes"* is the one regarding forgiving yourself. However, even here, what is really being conveyed is acceptance of the past and the necessity of merciful, loving self-care. Therefore, my advice would be to leave the term forgiveness out of the quote completely then reword it in a more self-affirming way that places no conditions on how we handle abuse, wrongdoing, or oppression.

I offer this a possible revision of the famous quote, as I penned in my journal and which incorporates the concept of moving on that Oprah was trying to convey: *You will begin to heal when you let go of thinking the past could be any different, when you realize those who wronged you have no power over you or your self-worth, and when you learn to be patient, loving, and merciful with yourself on the sometimes painful path to emotional wholeness and self-love.*

Victims Don't Need a 'Good Reason' To Not Forgive

When discussing justifiable reasons to not forgive, I think it is important to preface this by saying (as alluded to earlier in the context of God giving victims full right to choice): Anyone who is a victim of wrongdoing can—with or without a discernable reason—choose to *not* forgive the abuser, oppressor, or wrongdoer. The only required condition to this choice is that a wrongdoing has actually taken place. Other than that, victims don't need any justification for their choice, and we certainly don't have the right to demand that they explain themselves to us. If we believe a wrongdoing has not taken place, then this is another issue entirely and is not the subject of this book.

However, even in cases where we feel victims are overreacting to the circumstance, as long as they have indeed been wronged and have not transgressed anyone's rights, we are not allowed to take any pathway of blame against them. When wrongdoing occurs on any level, it is completely irrelevant to what degree *we* deem someone has actually suffered harm. More importantly, in the sight of God, it is not necessary that the wrongdoing be egregious before it is considered a wrongdoing. Again, the only condition to the right of a victim to choose non-forgiveness is that the wrongdoing has actually taken place—no matter how harmless, trivial, or insignificant it appears to an outsider looking in.

In the Qur'an, God makes this point undeniably clear when He refers to an incident of gossip and slander that harmed the reputation of a beloved wife of the Prophet (peace be upon him):

> "Behold, you received it on your tongues, and said out of your mouths things of which you had no knowledge. And you thought it to be a light matter, while it was most serious in the sight of Allah" (*An-Noor*, 24:15).

Therefore, when we are participating in trivializing someone else's suffering or accusing them of blowing things out of proportion while knowing full well they have indeed been wronged, let us reflect on the fact that what harms any innocent person on this earth is not a trivial matter to God. Furthermore, that harm includes the seemingly harmless pathways of blame that *we* take—often through what we say out of our mouths—against people who are wronging no one when they choose not to forgive.

Benefits of Discussing Good Reasons To Not Forgive

Though God has not placed on victims the burden of needing a "good reason" to not forgive, discussing justifiable reasons of non-forgiveness has numerous benefits. Here are three:

1. It helps survivors of abuse see in black-and-white the benefits of not forgiving and thus inspires validation and empowerment, should they choose to exercise this right.
2. It provides sincere advisors, counselors, friends, and loved ones with valuable information that can guide the advice, compassion, and support they offer survivors who either are conflicted on whether they should forgive or have already decided they will not.
3. It can aid in dismantling the culture of forced forgiveness or at least in reducing the number of well-meaning forgiveness peddlers who are genuinely unaware that not forgiving is sometimes more healing (and appropriate) than forgiving.

Some Good Reasons To Not Forgive

In a *Psychology Today* article entitled "6 Reasons Not to Forgive, Not Yet," author David Bedrick presents the following justifiable reasons to not forgive:

1. Urging forgiveness ignores the fact that anger naturally rises after being hurt and often needs to be integrated, not rooted out like some bacteria-borne illness.
2. Encouraging people to let go of anger before the natural course of its process is suppressive and harmful.
3. Counseling people to forgive when an injury is still recent risks dismissing the pain people are going through.
4. Advising forgiveness can ignore the value of confronting an offender.
5. The appropriateness of advising forgiveness depends upon who is asking whom to forgive.
6. Advising forgiveness, or letting go, to *groups* of people who have suffered sustained injustice is often ignorant and highly suspect.

Regarding number 4, Bedrick says:

What if I told you that forgiving too readily makes it more likely that those who hurt you will hurt you again? This is exactly what professor James K. McNulty found—that partners who forgave their partners easily were almost twice as likely to be mistreated soon afterwards.

Further, confronting your offender may not only make your life better, it can also make the world safer for others. Simply put, bullying, abuse, assault, and discrimination can be abated, although not eliminated, by confrontation.

One person I spoke with said: "Even at a very basic level, calling someone out on what they did to hurt others, is one way to make those changes. So many injustices happen because no one says anything about them" (September 2014).

In other words, much injustice and wrongdoing continue in both our personal lives and the world precisely because sufferers are continuously led to believe that forgiveness is always the right choice.

Unburdening, Not Forgiving

As any reputable mental health professional will tell you, a crucial part of supporting the healing process for any person is to listen to their expression of pain without passing judgment or adding commentary, then validate what they are feeling. The problem with forced forgiveness is that it requires both invalidating a survivor's feelings and subsequently passing judgment as a means of encouraging healing, specifically for those who are not ready (or willing) to forgive. Regarding this insensitive, harmful approach, trauma and relationship expert, Anastasia Pollock, says in her article "Why I Don't Use the Word 'Forgiveness' in Trauma Therapy":

> The people I work with in the therapy room are resilient and courageous. They are able to work through their traumas, but many get caught up on one point: They believe they are supposed to forgive the perpetrator but can't seem to get there.
> This is what I tell them: You don't have to forgive in order to move on.
> Understand that if a person comes in and finds that the word "forgiveness" resonates, I do not discourage it. We roll with it. But often people struggle with this word, and rightfully so. They do not want to imply what happened to them was in any way OK. They don't want to excuse the perpetrator's behavior. They feel the perpetrator is not deserving of forgiveness. The worst thing I can do as a therapist is to talk people out of the way they feel (GoodTherapy.org, January 2016).

In offering a more healing-centered word than *forgiveness*, Pollock echoes some of the sentiments expressed in the article "The 5 Faults With Forgiveness" by Sherrie Campbell, PhD, who says: "In acceptance the healing is about you. In forgiveness the healing is about the perpetrator" (HuffingtonPost.com, December 2014). Specifically, Pollock prefers the term *unburdening* over *forgiveness*. She says:

> Once we have determined that forgiveness is not necessary, we work on finding a word that will be more congruent for the person in his or her trauma work. I like the word unburdening,

which is something I first heard in Richard Schwartz's book *Internal Family Systems Therapy*. I understand unburdening as a letting-go process. That is, letting go of the power the trauma has over a person, expressing and releasing anger and other strong emotions about what happened without criticism or expectation of what needs to come next. (January 2016).

She then reiterates the importance of refraining from pushing forgiveness as a response to injustice, abuse, or wrongdoing, no matter how well-meaning we may be: "…trying to get someone who has been violated to forgive can feel like being victimized all over again" (January 2016).

14

Toxic Negativity in Extreme Positivity

"'I love everyone!'" Till today, hearing this gives me anxiety, no matter who says it. I've never known anyone to say this except that they caused so much hurt and harm, to me and others. And the only thing that this false belief guaranteed was that there was no self-reflection or self-correction afterward. For 'love' needs neither analysis nor change. It is always good and right—at least in the eyes of those who claim it excessively. So when I hear this, I know it really means, 'I'm always good, and I'm always right. And I'll entertain no other possibility.'"
—excerpt of *PAIN: From the Journal of Umm Zakiyyah*

◆

I lived for years in a form of suffering that I now think of as an abusive relationship with myself. Like so many other abusive relationships, continuously subjecting myself to harm each day nearly cost me my life. When I reached the point where I genuinely believed I *needed* to take my own life, I realized that there was a level of emotional wounding that I had yet to fathom.

Some religious people would trivialize or dismiss my suicidality as being sinful or rooted in the influences of *Shaytaan*. In other words, they would say I was experiencing this urge due to my weak faith, my human propensity to disobey God, or my listening to whispers of the devil. While I certainly recognize that some trauma and mental health struggles deem a person unaccountable for their actions in front of God, I do not mention my suicidality and emotional wounding to suggest that I am in this category.

I have no idea if I would have been excused or forgiven had I followed through with the urge. My mentioning of emotional wounding as the root of this struggle is for the purpose of pinpointing the *reason* behind the battle, not to suggest that I had an *excuse* if I'd lost it. As with all realities dealing with a person's true spiritual state and internal conflicts, I leave ultimate judgment to God, whether it concerns my soul or anyone else's. Thus, the point I'm making here is not that we can use emotional wounding as an excuse for any trial, but that we should see the trial as a warning sign pointing to internal wounds that need to be acknowledged and addressed. However, we cannot do this unless we seek to understand where the wounding originated in the first place.

Even in a case where a person is undoubtedly being influenced by the devil, this influence should not to be trivialized. Rather it should be understood. In my journal, I reflect on the importance of understanding more than trivializing: *Satan cannot reach us unless there's an opening. So when we face our human weaknesses and sins, let's not dismiss them by saying, "That's Shaytaan"—but instead focus on finding the opening in ourselves and lives that allowed him in.*

Put another way, even if we believe that all suicidality stems from the influences of the devil, this belief does not remove our responsibility to understand why a particular pathway of influence affects us more than others. Otherwise, what's the point of identifying the influence of the devil at all? All human beings are influenced by forces of both good and evil, and our challenge in life is to align ourselves as far as possible with the good. Thus, anyone who understands the complexity of life would never view any source of harm as trivial, whether we call it the devil or something else.

Personally, what I ultimately uncovered beneath my suicidal urge was emotional wounding that originated from living a life of self-abuse since childhood. However, before that suicidal moment, I understood my self-abuse as embracing a life of optimism, forgiveness, and striving to be a good Muslim. In other words, I was experiencing firsthand the destructive outcome of extreme positivity: toxic negativity.

The Negativity Must Point Somewhere

When I say *extreme positivity*, I mean the mental and emotional state of viewing nearly all ostensibly positive emotions and expressions as categorically "good" and viewing nearly all ostensibly negative emotions and expressions as categorically "bad." If a person who ascribes to extreme positivity believes in God, he or she will assume that God is pleased with "positivity" and that He is displeased with "negativity."

In the culture of forced forgiveness, we see one of the many dysfunctional branches of extreme positivity. In forced forgiveness, sufferers are taught that their pain is effectively a punishment from God for not being "positive" (i.e. forgiving the abuser or wrongdoer). Thus, they are cursed to live out life with angry, bitter hearts until they submit to extreme positivity by *always* absolving any abuser or wrongdoer for accountability for his or her actions.

In order to understand the toxic, destructive nature of extreme positivity in all of its forms, we must first understand the nature of creation itself. Nearly all faith traditions and spiritual ideologies recognize the inherent duality of human life: hot/cold, dry/wet, up/down, right/left, feminine/masculine, pleasure/pain, ease/hardship, happiness/sadness, tolerance/intolerance, love/hate, and so on. This duality is referred to in different terms depending on the spiritual ideology or faith tradition.

In Chinese philosophy this duality is referred to as the "yin and yang" of existence. In Islamic tradition, this duality is referred to in various terms depending on the context. In the subject of *qadr* (which was discussed in brief earlier), this duality is referred to as the *khayr* and *sharr* of what is divinely decreed or predestined for all life. In simplistic terms, *khayr* refers to our positive experiences, and *sharr* refers to our negative experiences. These terms also refer to the good/evil duality in life.

Regarding the nature of creation itself, Islamic tradition refers to this inherent duality in the concept of everything being created in pairs. The Qur'an says what has been translated to mean: "And of everything We have created pairs, that you may receive instruction [or be reminded]" (*Adh-Dhaariyaat*, 51:49).

Those who ascribe to extreme positivity reject the inherent duality of life (or at least the goodness in it). Thus, they seek the positive in nearly every circumstance, even when the positive is not appropriate or healthy. Proponents of extreme positivity also live in denial of the inevitable negative and sometimes evil consequences of their words, actions, and choices, even when they are wronging or harming others. Any person of faith who has been accosted, slandered, or abused by those who claim to call for "tolerance" but who are really calling for the criminalization of religion knows on a deeply personal level the toxic negativity that extreme positivity produces.

Undoubtedly, the subject of extreme positivity is vast, but for the purposes of this book, it is sufficient to say this: Whenever we resist, deny, or run away from the inevitable negativity in life, that negativity does not disappear. It simply points in a direction that we refuse to see, admit, or take responsibility for. Sometimes that hidden (or denied) negativity harms ourselves; other times it harms others. However, no matter what we *think* is happening, whenever we choose positivity, the negative aspect of the positive/negative duality must point *somewhere*.

In my case, my self-abuse meant that I continuously harmed myself in the name of honoring and respecting others. My extreme positivity had created a toxic mental and emotional environment for my spirit-soul because of the positive/negative duality inherent in my "always see and choose the good" approach to life.

As I sought to be a loving, forgiving person and a "good Muslim," I pointed all of my positive energy, assumptions, and love toward others—even in obvious cases of abuse and wrongdoing—and thus inadvertently pointed all negativity toward myself. Thus, it only makes sense that my "extreme positivity" ultimately resulted in emotional wounding that led to the next logical step of "positive" self-sacrifice: remove my negative, harm-filled existence from the world.

Healing Isn't in Positivity, It Is in Submission

At the center of all humans' dual experiences is the soul, which was created by God and will be returned to Him after it leaves its earthly shell. Thus, the human soul does not find ultimate peace or healing by aligning with only what is positive in life. It finds ultimate peace and healing by aligning with what reflects its divine purpose. This divinely assigned purpose is sometimes manifested in positive experiences and choices, and it is sometimes manifested in negative experiences and choices. However, in each divinely inspired alignment, the human submits to the *center* of its being—its soul's purpose—which is neither exclusively positive nor negative in earthly experience. In Islamic tradition, this "center of being" is *emaan* (authentic spirituality) as found in submission to Allah.

Those who ascribe to manmade life paths that contradict authentic spirituality will always be at odds with this divinely centered purpose, even when they imagine they are always choosing love, tolerance, and forgiveness. As discussed in brief earlier, when people ascribe to a culture of extreme positivity (such as forced forgiveness) and thus recognize no justifiable or necessary reason to *ever* not forgive, their chances of being continuously subjected to injustice, wrongdoing, and abuse increase tremendously.

Therefore, it should come as no surprise, as alluded to earlier in the context of Black people's misguided obligation to always forgive, that oppressive systems love influential personalities that call for love and forgiveness, but vilify influential personalities that call for justice and defending the oppressed. For this reason, historical figures like Malcolm X (El-Hajj Malik El-Shabazz) are less celebrated than non-threatening figures like Mohandas Gandhi and Martin Luther King, Jr. (who, not coincidentally, was assassinated shortly after he began vocalizing regrets for his singular approach to social justice).

Moreover, it is no accident that these oppressive systems require love and forgiveness only from those they continuously harm, but not from themselves as the oppressors. In other words, by establishing a one-sided culture of forced love and forgiveness (no matter how egregious their own crimes), oppressors ensure that their systems of hate and injustice will never be meaningfully challenged. In this, oppressors want the sufferers to believe that defending oneself against hate and injustice is a manifestation of hate and injustice itself.

Though nothing could be further from the truth, the brainwashing of the masses into accepting extreme positivity (which includes the culture of forced forgiveness) as the *only* way of life makes it impossible to discern harmful negativity from beneficial negativity, and harmful positivity from beneficial positivity.

True healing, whether on a personal or national scale, can only occur when the proper duality of human existence is embraced as a fundamental right of every human soul. Yes, as a general rule, we are most closely aligned with our soul's divine purpose in environments of love, tolerance, and forgiveness. However, there are moments that courageously standing up in the face of injustice, oppression, or abuse is healthier spiritually and practically than choosing "extreme positivity."

In the Qur'an, God says what has been translated to mean:

> "O you who believe! Stand out firmly for justice, as witnesses to Allah, even as against yourselves, your parents, your kin, and whether it be [against] rich or poor. For Allah can best protect both. So follow not the lusts [of your hearts], lest you may avoid justice. And if you distort [justice] or decline to do justice, verily Allah is well-acquainted with all that you do" (*An-Nisaa*, 4:135).

In cultures of extreme positivity, the lusts of our hearts which prevent ultimate justice can at times be our inclination to avoid negativity altogether.

Toxic Entitlement in Forgiveness Culture

Today, forgiveness peddling has become so widespread that abusers and wrongdoers themselves demand the extreme positivity it incites, specifically toxic negativity in the form of toxic entitlement. Because forced forgiveness links one's personal internal goodness and emotional wellbeing to forgiving abusers and wrongdoers (a manifestation of extreme positivity), it only naturally follows that *anyone* can now remind the sufferer of the threat of this cursed reality. Consequently, those involved in inflicting the emotional wounding itself feel emboldened to demand that their victims hand over their "get out of jail free" card.

If the victims don't hand out forgiveness on demand, the abusers now have every right (according to extreme positivity and forced forgiveness ideology) to tell their victims that they will pay with angry hearts and self-destructive bitterness. In the true definition of forgiveness—the one given to us by God—there is no requirement for all anger and blame to be gone from one's heart before one decides to forgive, and there is no threat of toxic anger and bitterness afflicting the heart if one exercises his or her option to not forgive. More importantly, irrespective of what is happening in a victim's heart, under no circumstances does an abuser or wrongdoer have the right to *demand* forgiveness.

When Toxic Negativity Points Toward God

One of the most spiritually destructive results of extreme positivity and forced forgiveness ideology is when humans attribute positivity to themselves and negativity to God. This happens either consciously or unconsciously, and it generally stems either from a manmade system of spirituality, or from a partial or complete rejection of authentic spirituality altogether.

Two popular manifestations of this anti-God toxic negativity are atheism and anger with (or disagreement with) God. This is undoubtedly a vast topic that warrants an entire book itself. However, in brief, we can understand these manifestations as follows: Both are forms of toxic negativity rooted in extreme positivity, which in its non-extreme, healthy form merely stems from the *fitrah*, that inherent spiritual nature and recognition of God that is imprinted on every spirit-soul.

In this *fitrah*, the human soul knows that its Creator is (among other things) Just and Merciful. Thus, whenever the human hears about God, the spirit-soul is at peace when the information complements the *fitrah*'s inherent knowledge of His Justice and Mercy. However, two things happen during the spirit-soul's sojourn on earth that cause natural positivity to morph into extreme positivity (and thus toxic negativity):
1. The spirit-soul is exposed to corrupt and inauthentic concepts of God and spirituality (often from the mouths and lives of those who claim to devoutly believe in Him).
2. The spirit-soul gradually begins to trust only its perceptions of the world (even regarding matters of the unseen) and what it feels should be gained materially and spiritually on

earth.

Naturally, for a person engaged in daily nourishment of the spirit-soul through authentic spirituality, any exposure to corrupt or inauthentic spirituality merely inspires the person to remove himself or herself from the toxic environment that is confusing the *fitrah* of the spirit-soul. The authentically spiritual person will further be inspired to focus on what the *fitrah* knows of God, not what corrupt humans have done while using His Name. This is because the *fitrah* inherently knows that Reality neither changes nor disappears simply because the word *reality* is often used outside of its proper context and understanding.

However, for soon-to-be atheists experiencing number 1, they do not guard the spirit-soul from these environments, nor do they tap into the *fitrah's* "common sense" understanding of Reality. Thus, they become spiritually corrupt themselves. They then borrow from the definition of God that they know from the *fitrah* and compare it to the "reality" of God they see in "real life" (i.e. the toxic "realities" they are exposed to), then conclude that God does not exist because this toxic reality contradicts the Reality of God's Justice and Mercy. Ironically, it is their spirit-soul's inherent knowledge of God's existence and His flawless attributes of Justice and Mercy that even allow atheists to reject Reality at all.

Though atheists also fall into the pitfalls of number 2 (trusting only their own perceptions of and experiences with the world), pitfall 2 chiefly defines people who believe in God (or a Higher Being) but reject all or part of authentic spirituality. In their efforts to make sense of the material and/or spiritual world sans the toxic "realities" they witness, they adjust their definition of Reality such that they distance themselves as far as possible from what they *think* is at the root of the spiritual corruption and widespread harm they see. Furthermore, when true Reality contracts their heart's desires, they redefine Reality such that their heart's desires are met (even if only in their imagination). When they know their desires contradict Reality, they become angry with God or openly disagree with Him. This results in efforts to redefine how Reality *should* be. Ultimately, the end result of number 2 is the rejection of authentic spirituality and putting a manmade spiritual path in its place.

In justifying these manmade spiritual systems, these anti-God people (who claim to believe in God or a Higher Being) draw on their extreme positivity model and thus point to number 1 (negative behavior of "religious" people) as an excuse for their innovated life path. By claiming that humans' concepts of God and "organized religion" are negative and corrupt, they argue that traditional religious Reality needs an extreme makeover or outright rejection. In doing this, they merely introduce to the world a new "organized religion," which if practiced by human beings (the only possibility) will over time witness obvious negativity and widespread corruption—as is already happening in the forced forgiveness culture.

The reality of toxic negativity and widespread corruption is inevitable in *any* life path practiced by humans because the root of all widespread harm and corruption is the human heart. Thus, we can change our spiritual path and religious affiliation a zillion times over (and we can even remove "religion" from the face of the earth entirely) and the world would still be plagued with widespread harm and corruption—until humans make the conscious choice to change the condition of themselves by rooting out the pollution in their hearts.

In Islamic tradition this fact is addressed in many verses of the Qur'an, but here is one of the most famous: "Allah will not change the condition of a people until they change what is in themselves" (*Ar-Ra'd*, 13:11). The word that is being translated as *themselves* is the Arabic term *anfusihim,* which refers to the heart-spirit-soul essence of humans.

However, as the culture of forced forgiveness and extreme positivity has made painfully obvious—especially in its devastating effects on black slaves historically and on systems of abuse and oppression currently—this purification of the heart-spirit-soul can never be successful without authentic spirituality. In authentic spirituality, we have a balanced, self-correction approach to life that emphasizes love, peace, tolerance, and forgiveness as a general rule, but also emphasizes the need for justice and standing up against wrongdoing and oppression when necessary. It also allows for the healthy, natural duality of life that prioritizes self-care over self-harm and balances both positivity and negativity wherever one is more appropriate and healthier for the spirit-soul and circumstance.

Forced Forgiveness and Toxic Entitlement Toward God

In understanding the spiritually destructive harms that toxic negativity produces, it is relevant to mention the forced forgiveness and toxic entitlement that some "religious" people ascribe to under the guise of having a positive definition of faith. In this form of extreme positivity, a person's forced forgiveness and toxic entitlement ideology is directed at God himself. Like those who ascribe to number 2 above (i.e. trusting only their own thoughts and conclusions about the world), these people exhibit an extreme positivity that manifests as anger with God or disagreement with Him, specifically regarding who should or should not be forgiven, and who should or should not be granted Paradise.

These people's underlying mentality mirrors the toxic entitlement of abusers and wrongdoers who demand forgiveness from those who, in reality, owe them nothing. In their self-serving concept of faith and spirituality, they imagine that God is here to heed their desires and demands, and not the other way around. Therefore, if they perceive that they or someone they love is not getting what they "deserve," whether materially or spiritually, they accuse God of being unjust and unmerciful.

In truth, God owes humans nothing at all while humans owe God everything. Allah, the Creator of all, is the Provider of our very being and existence while we are the provider of absolutely nothing—except from what He himself has given us. However, some of us still manage to use these very gifts of life, speech, and thought to rage against the One who has given them to us. Thus, due to feeling that we (or our loved ones) have been denied something we "deserve," we openly criticize His rules, decrees, and principles of material and spiritual reward.

In anti-religion crowds, this raging is sometimes against the idea of God having any spiritual requirements at all before a human can enter Paradise. [Meanwhile, humans themselves have scores of worldly requirements that they put in place before anyone can touch or enjoy anything *they* own (which was incidentally given to them by God).] In those who claim to accept religion, this raging is sometimes against the same concept when they have decided that a specific individual "deserves" forgiveness or Paradise. In this, if they perceive that someone they love does not (or will not) fulfill the spiritual requirements to enter Paradise or to be forgiven, they deduce that it is God who is wrong and not the person who *chooses* to reject Him.

Ironically, instead of inviting the person they love to authentic spirituality (and thus true forgiveness), they rage against the idea that authentic spirituality should matter to God at all. This, despite the fact that (by definition) rejecting authentic spirituality is denying the rights of God. However, just like the toxic entitlement of abusers and wrongdoers who demand forgiveness from those whose rights they violated, these people violate the rights of God—then they tap into their toxic negativity and entitlement to demand forgiveness when they haven't even made *efforts* to deserve it. In this, they imagine that they can use the same manipulation techniques of forced forgiveness that they use on humans when demanding undeserved gifts from God.

15

Good Anger, Bad Anger

"I came to see that a lot more elements contributed to becoming a happy and well-rounded person. Anger, it turned out, wasn't a bad thing. Instead it was the key to emotional freedom."
—Andrea Brandt, *Mindful Anger: A Pathway to Emotional Freedom*

◆

When I was trapped in a cycle of self-abuse, I continuously punished myself for *any* expression of anger, and this naturally only exacerbated my emotional wounding. Because I was unknowingly rejecting the divinely decreed duality of life, my "extreme positivity" led me to repeatedly harm myself as I sought to be exclusively positive to others. I had mistakenly understood praiseworthy self-sacrifice for others as self-inflicted suffering toward myself.

Once I began to heal emotionally, I came to understand that praiseworthy self-sacrifice in the service of others naturally enhances your "center of being." It does not deplete it, harm it or compromise it. In other words, if we are involved in healthy self-sacrifice, our authentic spirituality is nourished, not starved. When we are feeling drained and emotionally depleted in our service to others, we are not drawing from our sincere spiritualty; we are drawing from something else (usually others' demands and expectations of us that do not reflect what we truly want or believe).

In my book *Pain. From the Journal of Umm Zakiyyah*, I reflect on the importance of self-care in sacrifice: "Suffering is not the same as sacrifice. Know yourself. Know your limits. Draw the line." I also share this realization that came to me after years of suffering self-abuse:

> You cannot give of a self that does not exist. Thus, self-care and self-preservation must be essential to your life if you wish to

truly give of yourself to others. You cannot give charity from wealth that does not encompass your possessions, and you cannot give from a spirit that does not encompass your being. So invest in your emotional, physical, and spiritual wealth. You can only spend from what you have (2016).

In this vein, when we are deciding whether or not to forgive, it is important that we understand that forgiveness might involve *some* level of sacrifice, but forgiveness should never result in suffering. When forgiveness involves more emotional suffering than healing, then perhaps it is not time or healthy to forgive. In this, it is important to realize that some negativity (such as choosing to not forgive) has positive and beneficial functions in our lives. Healthy negativity rejuvenates parts of us that were lost or damaged during emotional wounding. Healthy anger is one manifestation of this "positive negativity."

Embracing Positive Negativity

Spiritually, the problem we face when embracing only positive feelings and experiences and rejecting negative ones (such as anger and not forgiving), is that we imply, as Pete Walker discusses in the book *The Tao of Fully Feeling,* that God is present for us only in our positive experiences in life, not in our negative ones.

In comprehending ostensibly "negative" choices such as not forgiving, it is important to understand that "negative" is not always synonymous with "evil" and that "positive" is not always synonymous with "good." In fact, feelings like pain and anguish can be the epitome of compassion, goodness, and mercy, particularly when they fall under the concept of *empathy*. In Islamic tradition, this profound point is conveyed in the following famous prophetic hadith:

> "The example of the believers in their affection, mercy, and compassion for each other is that of a body. When any limb aches, the whole body reacts with sleeplessness and fever" (Bukhari and Muslim).

Those who try to consistently feel positive, happy, and pain-free are susceptible not only to denial and repressed anger but also to apathy, cowardice, and selfishness. In my book *Pain. From the Journal of Umm Zakiyyah*, I reflect on the chilling effect of the idea that kindness and compassion are found only in happiness and forgiveness:

> Sometimes getting upset is the highest form of kindness and compassion. Imagine someone wrongs you or your child in the most vicious way, and your friends and loved ones rush to the wrongdoer, all smiles and hugs, saying "We love you so much!" while treating *you* harshly, saying you should get over it and forgive. "What hurts her hurts me" is what the Prophet (peace be upon him) would say about his daughter. But today, when a believer is wronged, we're effectively told of the wrongdoers, "What hurts *them* hurts me" (2016).

I mention all of this to say that any emotionally healthy and spiritually mature person who chooses not to forgive is doing so as a result of seeking some greater good or positivity from that choice—even if nothing more than the internal affirmation that they have a right to that choice. Thus, for them, not forgiving is not "negative" or damaging; rather it is positive and healing.

But why would you want to live with all that anger and bitterness? many people ask. In this inquiry (which is really just a thinly veiled pathway of blame aimed at harming victims), there is the failure to distinguish between good anger and bad anger, or more specifically healthy anger and unhealthy anger. Though this topic was touched on briefly in earlier chapters, I want to highlight it here for people of faith who have used the "extreme positivity" model to interpret spiritual instructions to avoid anger. In other words, due to their lack of understanding of the healthy, inevitable duality of life (specifically anger/contentment), they view all expressions of anger as sinful and bad.

I explain the difference between healthy anger and sinful anger in the following excerpt from my book, *Reverencing the Wombs That Broke You*:

> When professionals suggest the healthy release of anger, they are not speaking of what many religions consider sinful anger. There is a difference between healthy anger in response to an upsetting situation and unhealthy anger that leads one to harm the self and

others...

In Islamic tradition, when a man came to the Prophet (peace be upon him) asking for advice, he told the man three times, "Do not get angry" (Bukhari and Muslim). However, in other narrations, the Prophet himself is being described as becoming angry. For example, when a Muslim argued with a Jew and claimed the Prophet Muhammad was better than Prophet Moses (peace be upon them), the Prophet is described as becoming angry until anger was apparent on his face. He then said, "Do not give superiority to any prophet [over another] amongst God's prophets..." (Bukhari).

Naturally, these varying advices and circumstances point to the necessity of differentiating between healthy expressions of anger and unhealthy expressions of anger. In mental health, one of the healthiest expressions of anger is when a survivor of abuse turns a breaking point, such as an emotional implosion, into a breakthrough. A breakthrough occurs when the survivor begins the journey of conscious healing of the spirit through self-care, which is manifested in self-honesty and self-protection (2017).

The Challenge of Embracing Healthy Negativity

I can understand how the topic of healthy anger can be scary. It was a terrifying topic for me for quite some time, even after I began my journey of healing. It is much easier (theoretically speaking) to view all anger as harmful and thus stay away from it. After all, if we take the risk of embracing healthy anger, how can we protect ourselves from falling into unhealthy or toxic anger, which harms ourselves and others?

As with any path of healing, healthy anger is about striving for perfection, not about actualizing perfection. Practically speaking, embracing healthy anger is about the daily practice of aligning with one's "center of being," which is attained through mindful choices that support one's emotional and spiritual health. The goal in these mindful (or heart-centered) choices is that everything we say or do ensures that our spirit-soul is properly nourished. This nourishment includes expressions of both positivity and negativity, where appropriate.

When (not if) we err or fall out of proper alignment with our soul's purpose, we should engage in patient, merciful self-care by using authentic spirituality to repent and seek forgiveness from the Creator of the human soul. As we seek to right our wrongs, it is important that we understand the tremendous blessing in being endowed with the spiritual insight to even recognize and subsequently self-correct emotional imbalance, human error, or deliberate sin. In this vein, healing is achieved through sincerity, self-correction, patience, and gratitude—as defined by and practiced through authentic spirituality.

One of the biggest challenges we face in achieving full emotional healing is the assumption that emotional or spiritual health is a static, achievable goal. In truth, emotional or spiritual health is a daily process that we must commit to every waking moment. Thus, full emotional healing is only "full" because it involves unabated, continuous *striving* for emotional wellness. Emotional healing is not something that we can tick off as "completed" one day then move on to something else. While certain *aspects* of emotional healing can indeed be fully achieved and completed, every success in the spirit-soul experience merely introduces us to a new challenge (and level) of the spirit-soul journey.

For this reason, the only path to emotional and spiritual success is in humble submission to the sometimes excruciatingly difficult daily work involved in what is called in Islamic tradition *jihaad-al-nafs*. This Arabic term can be translated as the continuous internal battle of the heart-spirit-soul against itself as it works toward the goal of spiritual health at death. It is this internal battle that represents the very foundation of sincerity in authentic spirituality, which encompasses true faith. For this reason, I penned in my journal this reflection on the very definition of faith itself: *Islam is submission, yes. But it is more than that. It is a relentless fight till death—against oneself—to save one's soul.*

In committing to the lifelong internal battle against oneself for spiritual height, what is key is the daily practice of humility, patience, and perseverance. In guarding ourselves against giving up or falling into self-deception, we must avoid the seductions of instant gratification and manmade spirituality. Both are harmful addictions that often are offshoots of extreme positivity.

Just as we face addictions to instant gratification in seeking to achieve physical beauty without the daily work, we face addictions to instant gratification in seeking to achieve emotional and spiritual beauty without the daily work. In the physical realm, we do whatever allows us to lose weight and look good for the moment, even if it means failing health in the long term. Likewise, in the emotional or spiritual realm, we do whatever allows us to *feel* good and claim to have hearts free or anger and blame for the moment, even if it means failing emotional and spiritual health in the long term—or living a "positive" and "happy" life rooted in denial, repressed anger, and self-deception.

Thus, whenever we seek inspiration and guidance from others on our spiritual journeys, we must be sure that we are not embracing a path that will ultimately lead to more harm than good at the end of our spirit-soul's journey in this world.

16
Reclaiming the Beauty of Forgiveness

"Why do you hesitate to turn to your Lord? Why do you not bend your knees in prayer or rest your head on the ground, prostrating in humility? Why do you not raise your hands, begging with tears in your eyes? 'I don't deserve mercy and forgiveness!' you say. And you're right. None of us do. But that's the goal of life in the end—to be granted the mercy and forgiveness that none of us deserve.'
—Umm Zakiyyah, lessons from *Hearts We Lost*

◆

I spent all of my childhood and most of my adulthood overlooking faults, making excuses for people, and forgiving wrongs done to me. Till today I maintain: *If someone sincerely wants God's forgiveness, then they certainly have mine.* Even if someone realizes only after I die the wrongs they have done to me, so long as they sincerely repent, I forgive them, *insha'Allah*.

In my journal I wrote these words inspired by a deeply moving conversation I had with one of my sisters: *If I should ever pass from this world while you are left behind, know that time and distance, and even our misunderstandings and disagreements, never erased from my heart the love and appreciation I have for you in my life. My greatest fear upon death, other than my own soul, is that those left behind will live in agony for any wrong they think they've done to me. So if you're reading this, know that you are forgiven and I love and appreciate you, even if I never had the words or the wisdom to tell you while I was with you in this world.*

I wrote this heartfelt entry just months before I felt compelled to take my own life. Till today, reading it inspires tears in my eyes. I am moved by both my raw sincerity and my unhesitant embracing of forgiveness. But in my tears is also grief that is bittersweet. In those words, I see the naïve, desperate girl sending out enduring love to those who have hurt her, in hopes that some of that love would find its way back to her. Months later, I came to the heart-crushing realization that it would not, at least not from the spirit-souls who mattered most to me at the time.

It was after this heartbreaking realization and my subsequent brush with suicidality that I penned this somber entry in my journal: *The apology is not coming. The regret is not coming. And the love is not coming. What now? You still have your own life to lead.*

Painful Healing

Thus far, my healing journey has been the most difficult, agonizing emotional trial of my life. It has also been one of the loneliest. But it has also been one of the most empowering and rewarding experiences I have ever had. During this painful journey, I've come to understand love like I never have before. I have been blessed with companions and loved ones I didn't even know existed. And I've experienced a level of happiness and joy I didn't know was possible in this earthly life. So even as I was emotionally abandoned by those I thought loved and cared for me, they were replaced by spirit-souls who were exponentially better for my life and soul.

By the mercy of God, I have made tremendous improvements, in my emotional health, and amongst them is fully embracing forgiveness as a divinely gifted choice and subsequently understanding that my emotional healing is not dependent on it. Nevertheless, I continuously choose forgiveness as a general rule, but I make far more exceptions than I previously gave myself permission to.

I still have moments of hurt, blame, and anger, especially regarding what incited such deep emotional wounding that I felt I didn't even have the right to be alive. However, these angry moments are much less intense than when I first began uncovering my repressed anger. My physical health has also improved, and though I still have emotional triggers, they are not as debilitating as they used to be. I still seek beneficial sources of healing, but as far as I am able, I stay away from environments of forced forgiveness, toxic entitlement, and spiritual abuse. I do this not only to preserve my emotional health, but also to preserve the beautiful meaning of forgiveness in my heart.

Being constantly subjected to emotional manipulation, guilt trips, and spiritual abuse in the context of forced forgiveness resulted in the word *forgiveness* itself becoming an emotional trigger for me. Till today it is difficult for me to stomach quotes and speeches focusing more on the rights of the wrongdoer to receive forgiveness than on the rights of the harmed to be listened to, validated, and supported irrespective of whether or not they choose to forgive.

When the focus of blame is turned on the ones who are hurting—through the statement or implication that they are bad people for expressing their anger and hurt—I have to beseech my Lord for help in calming the conflagration of rage in my heart. Till today, it is difficult for me to wrap my mind around the default pathway of blame being directed at the harmed more than the harmers, especially when emotional healing or religious righteousness are used as the tools of manipulation and harm.

When people defend their blaming of the harmed by saying that everyone makes mistakes or that no one should be accosted for falling into human error, sin, or wrongdoing, I wonder why a victim's expressed anger and hurt almost never falls under the category of forgivable error, sin, or wrongdoing that these people say we must consistently excuse, ignore, or be patient with. What is it, I wonder, that causes the human heart to soften more toward abuse and wrongdoing than it does toward the anger and hurt incited by that abuse and wrongdoing?

I still don't have a satisfactory answer, except that I suspect the roots of this imbalance are in the cultures of forced forgiveness, privilege, and elitism. I say this because usually when the pathways of blame focus primarily (or only) on the victim, at least one of these three dysfunctional systems is in place.

Challenges To Preserving the Beauty of Forgiveness

In the system of forced forgiveness, it is only the wrongdoer who deserves immediate empathy, forgiveness, and absolution of wrongs—while the victim is punished with a heart full of anger and bitterness should he or she choose to not forgive.

In the system of privilege, only those who share superficial traits with those in power have the right to make mistakes or inflict harm without accountability—while victims are punished for the slightest show of defiance in the face injustice (let alone for actual crimes), or even for something as inconsequential as the refusal to forgive.

In the system of elitism (which is similar to that of privilege and often overlaps it), only certain categories of people are granted the right to full existence, as they are deemed inherently superior to others. Thus, it becomes an obligation upon "unimportant" and insignificant "commoners" to accept any harm inflicted upon them by the elite, without even the right to *expression* of hurt or anger.

In the culture of forced forgiveness is a dysfunctional manifestation of how emotional manipulation and harm are utilized in so much mental health and life coaching today, even when the advisor has the best of intentions. This culture of forced forgiveness is also threaded throughout systems of privilege and elitism.

In the system of privilege, the culture of forced forgiveness is reflected in how anti-Black racism in the United States dictates zero tolerance for even the *appearance* of Black strength or "defiance" (even if only in a white person's imagination). Consequently, Black victims of murder by law enforcement are constantly blamed for their own deaths, even when they've committed no crime or posed no genuine threat to the officer's life. In contrast, in the name of forgiveness, Black people are continuously expected and required to forgive the numerous crimes committed against them.

Ironically, despite the culture of forced forgiveness that Black people are continuously held to—no matter how obvious or egregious the crime against them—their own crimes are not only *not* forgiven, they are viciously and unjustly punished. Moreover, these "real" crimes committed by some Black people are further used as a justification for the mistreatment and murder of Black people who have broken no laws. This oppressor-centered brand of forced forgiveness began in slavery and is now, unfortunately, widely embraced as a religious obligation amongst many sincere Black people.

In the system of elitism, which is manifested in both white privilege and religious hierarchies, people of lower status are taught to view their physical lives, emotional needs, and spiritual souls as inherently less valuable than those with a higher status (who allegedly have greater importance in front of God). Here, the culture of forced forgiveness mirrors the white-mandated version of the slaves' Christianity: In all things, the elite are superior and excused, even when harming, abusing, or wronging those "beneath" them. Thus, the "good person" of lowly status always forgives and treats the "superior" person with respect, deference, and honor, even in the face of any harm, abuse, or wrongdoing.

In religious elitism, showing respect to the religious elite is more fundamental than listening to, validating, or responding to the complaints of those who are harmed, abused, or wronged by the elite. Thus, before victims of wrongdoing are granted even the elusive *opportunity* to get help after being wronged, they must micromanage their word choice and voice tone so that the religious elite are unoffended and unharmed by any implications of wrongdoing.

In all things involving the religious elite, the starting point must be in the lowly person showing full respect, honor, and deference to his or her superiors. Thus, even in discussions of wrongdoing, the lowly are told that no matter what was done to them, offending or "disrespecting" the religious elite is a grave sin. If it is somehow ascertained that one of the elite is actually guilty of wrongdoing, the lowly person is guilted into immediately forgiving the transgression and subsequently maintaining full deference, honor, and "proper etiquette" when speaking about the one who wronged him or her.

In most cases, lowly "commoners" are told that, if they are indeed "people of faith," they wouldn't speak about the harm, abuse, or wrongdoing at all, especially in public. And they certainly wouldn't think that "one mistake" cancels out the superior station and immeasurable good done by the religious elite, who are "friends of God."

In Search of True Forgiveness

Naturally, these systems of manipulation, privilege, and injustice mar the beauty of true forgiveness. As a result, this marring makes it that much more difficult for survivors to healthily choose forgiveness, even when they want to. Thus, for those whose hearts wish to reclaim the beauty of forgiveness, it is important that they first understand what forgiveness is not before embracing what they think it is. This approach of negation-before-affirmation allows for the heart to be free of any emotional and spiritual pollutants before forgiveness takes its proper place.

Not coincidentally, this negation-before-affirmation approach mirrors the formal testimony of faith that is recited in Islamic tradition when the human heart is ready to embrace authentic spirituality (*emaan*). In Arabic, the one who is sincerely ready to submit to his or her soul's divine purpose recites, *Laa ilaaha illaAllaah*, which can be translated as "Nothing [and no one] has the right to be worshipped except God alone."

Scholars of authentic spirituality have on numerous occasions reflected on the divine wisdom behind this negation-before-affirmation approach. However, in brief, only after first negating any false spirituality that could contradict or corrupt the soul's noble purpose is the heart ready to truly tread the life path of faith and spiritual authenticity.

Similarly, authentic spirituality teaches that true forgiveness emanates from a sincere heart free of false or corrupted spiritual concepts taught under the umbrella of the term. At the same time, the Creator of the spirit-soul knows that the human heart is volatile and imperfect. Therefore, He does not require a perfect heart before it is deemed a forgiving heart. He requires only that the heart is sincere when forgiving. However, sincerity does not require a heart completely free from anger and blame. Not only is this nearly impossible, it is not necessarily healthy, particularly when the anger has a positive, functional purpose. What authentic spirituality purifies from the heart is toxic anger and blame, not natural anger and blame.

In this vein, we can understand that true forgiveness requires none of the following:

1. the obligation to forgive
2. a heart that no longer feels anger or blame
3. a spirit that feels no emotional pain or sadness
4. a life free of emotional triggers and other inevitable evidence of emotional wounding
5. the curse of toxic anger and bitterness if the person chooses to not forgive

What true forgiveness requires and affirms are <u>all</u> of the following:

1. free choice to make the decision without coercion or manipulation
2. sincerity
3. the promise of *extra* and *increased* reward (emotionally and spiritually) from God due to the voluntary choice
4. not seeking any worldly or spiritual punishment for the abuser on account of what he or she has done
5. freedom to protect oneself from further physical, emotional, or spiritual harm (i.e. there is no worldly or spiritual obligation to the wrongdoer on account of choosing forgiveness)

Freedom from the Burden of Perfection

Just as choosing forgiveness does not make our hearts suddenly immortal and free from the natural duality of emotional life, choosing forgiveness does not make us suddenly obligated to behave as if the abuse, harm, or wrongdoing never occurred. Forgiving is not forgetting, and forgiving is not subjecting oneself to harm, even if the harm is only psychological or emotional and incited by being in the presence of the abuser or wrongdoer.

In fact, forgiveness implies absolutely nothing except that the survivor will seek no worldly or spiritual retribution for the wrongdoer in response to the crime. Other than that, how the survivor chooses to live out his or her life following the choice of forgiveness is completely up to him or her. Some survivors choose to reconcile with those whom they have forgiven; others do not. Just as forgiveness itself is a free choice, so is life after forgiveness.

In supporting the freedom of choice following forgiveness, I share the following excerpts from my book *Pain. From the Journal of Umm Zakiyyah*, some of which are addressed to wrongdoers who have been forgiven but expect the survivor to act as if no harm was ever done:

> At a certain point, it really doesn't matter how much good someone has done for you. The wounds of betrayal, humiliation, and harm sometimes run so deep that they cut right through the very life veins of all previous good and happiness. So be careful. There are some things an "I'm sorry"—and even sincere repentance to God—cannot fix. A person may forgive you, and even God may forgive you. But that doesn't mean the person can handle your presence in their life ever again.

◆◆◆

> I think, if you've hurt someone deeply and you're really sorry, you should leave them alone. You should give them room and time to heal. Don't suffocate them with your presence. Don't try too hard to make it up to them. Because perhaps you can't. There are just some things you can't undo, some things people can't un-experience, and some things you just can't make right. So just ask the person for forgiveness, and ask God for forgiveness. Then leave them alone.

◆◆◆

> "Allah teaches us to forgive and overlook, but He also says the earth is spacious. So there are some people you forgive but move away from to preserve yourself."
> —reflections from my sister

17
When To Encourage Forgiveness

"If the child of Adam knew his account of every wrong he's done to himself and others, he wouldn't be so quick to become angry at others' wrongs toward him. Instead, he'd rush to forgive them in hopes that Allah would forgive him."
—excerpt of *FAITH. From the Journal of Umm Zakiyyah*

◆

When we fully understand the true definition of forgiveness and that no obligation exists in offering it, we can more safely discern when it is helpful to encourage forgiveness. And here, the operative word is *encourage*. Under no circumstances should an encouragement of forgiveness involve even the kindest or gentlest form of emotional manipulation, harm, or abuse.

Nevertheless, we are all in desperate need of God's mercy and forgiveness. For this reason, choosing forgiveness as a means to *increase* our reward in front of God and our chances of being forgiven for our own wrongs and misdeeds is beautiful and empowering.

In authentic spirituality, God encourages forgiveness. It is humans who force it. When God encourages forgiveness, He promises us increased reward and makes us mindful of our own sins and transgressions that we want forgiven. However, He does not threaten us with worldly, emotional, or spiritual punishment if we choose to not forgive, even if that punishment is merely toxic anger and bitterness lingering in our hearts.

Nevertheless, it is upon all of us to sincerely examine our hearts and determine whether or not we will benefit most from forgiving or not forgiving. While toxic anger and bitterness is not a guaranteed outcome of not forgiving, if we are not properly tending to our emotional and spiritual needs daily, what began as natural or even healthy anger and blame can morph and ferment into toxic anger and bitterness. Here is where some people have found the choice of sincere forgiveness helpful.

However, what is more important than choosing forgiveness to overcome toxic anger and bitterness is embracing authentic spirituality, specifically the pillar of *qadr*—humble and sincere acceptance that what happened in the past could not have transpired any differently. Other aspects of authentic spirituality that are more essential to emotional health than forgiveness are *sabr*, *shukr*, and *tawakkul*.

Sabr is often translated as *patience*, but more specifically it refers to holding oneself back from doing anything that harms the spirit-soul on its divinely assigned course of authentic spirituality, as well as remaining steadfast upon doing what is necessary to nourish the spirit-soul on this divinely assigned course.

Shukr is often translated as *gratefulness*, but more specifically it refers to not only a state of the heart but also one's words and actions that emanate from a place of love, appreciation, and reverence for the Creator. Practically, when a person does any act of goodness that purifies the spirit-soul due to the sincere love he or she has for the Creator, this is *shukr*.

Tawakkul is often translated as trust in God, but more specifically it refers to the heart's full acceptance of the past, present and future *qadr*, while having full faith that whatever God has in store for the spirit-soul is good for it, no matter how painful one's emotional and physical experiences are on earth. *Tawakkul* further includes the sincere and consistent actions a person does to bring about a desired outcome for one's life and soul, while fully trusting that God will either grant the soul's desire or bestow upon it something even greater and better than it initially imagined or hoped for.

It is only in the spiritually nourishing environments of *sabr*, *shukr*, and *tawakkul* that the essence of true forgiveness can be felt in the heart. Nevertheless, even if a person chooses to not forgive, any heart endowed with these three spiritual gifts would not be burdened with toxic anger and bitterness. Thus, when we believe that it is time to encourage a person to forgive, it is more important that we ensure that they have at least on a minimal level incorporated these aspects of authentic spirituality into their lives.

However, even when encouraging these three essential aspects of authentic spirituality (with or without forgiveness), it is important that we understand that the essence of *sabr*, *shukr*, and *tawakkul* is rooted in *jihaad-al-nafs* (the ongoing internal battle for spiritual purity within oneself) more than it is rooted in the perfect actualizing of these spiritual experiences. In other words, no matter how spiritually "pure" our hearts become, we will never overcome our humanity, nor should we be required to.

In my book, <u>*Faith. From the Journal of Umm Zakiyyah*</u>, I reflect on this crucial point, along with the proper understanding of natural positivity and negativity in life:

> *Shukr.*
> Remaining grateful doesn't necessarily mean always being positive, and being positive doesn't necessarily mean always feeling happy. Gratefulness is more a way of life rooted in faith in God than it is the experience of never feeling distressed about life's severe trials or negative circumstances. Yes, gratefulness requires a level of underlying positivity, but it doesn't require complete positivity. While negativity should never be allowed to define us, feeling moments of negativity is natural and unavoidable. This doesn't make you ungrateful. It makes you human.
> And one of the surest ways to destroy both gratefulness and happiness is to deny your right to being human.

I mention these reflections on authentic spirituality in the context of forgiveness because often when someone appears to "need" to forgive, what they really need is support in reconnecting with authentic spirituality, specifically as it relates to *qadr*, *sabr*, *shukr*, and *tawakkul*. But none of these spiritual experiences requires forgiving someone. Nevertheless, if the human heart embraces true forgiveness along with authentic spirituality, forgiveness becomes a means to further nourish, beautify, and enrich the spirit-soul.

Encouraging Forgiveness

It is only natural that when we see someone hurting and want the best for them, we are inclined to share with them the beauty, power, and enriching nature of forgiveness. However, even with the sincerest of intentions, it is important that we do not conflate emotional healing with forgiveness. No matter how emotionally healing forgiveness can indeed be for many people, forgiveness is not synonymous with emotional healing, and it is not a condition of it.

Thus, when we are tempted to rush to the subject of forgiveness when we see someone suffering emotionally, it is important to take a step back and determine whether or not what we really want for them can be achieved through some other means (at least for the time being). These alternate routes to alleviating emotional suffering include acceptance of the past and unburdening the heart (as discussed earlier), both of which are natural results of authentic spirituality rooted in *qadr*, *sabr*, *shukr*, and *tawakkul*.

However, there are possible exceptions in which the discussion of forgiveness could actually help the emotionally hurt person, even if he or she is at the beginning of the healing journey. I list five possible scenarios here:
1. when a person is irrationally angry and/or fails to distinguish between feeling hurt and being wronged (because all feelings of hurt and offense are not incited by actual wrongdoing)
2. when the wrongdoing is quite obviously equally shared between both parties (like two friends insulting each other in a moment of anger)
3. when the person is blind to having been guilty of identical or comparable transgressions or wrongs
4. when the mentioning of forgiveness enlightens the person to the opportunity of extra reward and blessings from God
5. when the person (without prompting or coercion) expresses a genuine desire to forgive or to consider the option for themselves

Here, I say that encouraging forgiveness in these five incidents can *help*—not heal—the person, as all help is not necessarily healing. However, even in these cases, we have to tread carefully because our perception of what is going on does not always reflect the reality of what is happening.

Emotional trauma is so complex that it is generally uncovered in layers, and often the person who has suffered it is not fully cognizant of what is beneath the surface. Thus, what often appears to us as someone's irrational anger, equally shared wrongdoing, or blindness to their own wrongs is actually just the manifestation of a single trigger or incident pointing to something much deeper. For this reason, we must tread very carefully even in circumstances in which a person appears to be overreacting, behaving irrationally, or unnecessarily blaming others.

In cases of sustained abuse, these "irrational" reactions are precisely what occur during emotional implosion, and these incidents are signs that uncovering the root of the emotional wounding is far more urgent than encouraging forgiveness. Once a survivor has moved along the path to recovery enough to recognize, acknowledge, and validate his or her underlying emotional wounding, forgiveness can be encouraged so long as it is not presented as a bargaining chip for emotional wellness.

Final Notes

◆

In discussing forgiveness in the context of emotional trauma, it is important to note that some trauma is suffered as a result of no actual wrongdoing on anyone's part. Some emotional suffering is purely incidental and based upon what God has decreed for the person through no fault of theirs or anyone else's. This book dealt with healing and forgiveness in the context of suffering obvious abuse, injustice, or wrongdoing, even if the one inflicting the harm would not define his or her actions as such.

Naturally, healing from incidental trauma is different from healing from trauma suffered as a result of the deliberate choice of someone else. However, all trauma requires emotional healing, and many aspects of emotional suffering present similar symptoms, irrespective of the source. In particular, anger and blame often surface in both types of trauma, even when there is no clear "target" of the anger and blame. For incidental based trauma, such as a loved one's death or illness, what is key is showing empathy and patience with the person's expression of pain and suffering.

In seeking to be sources of support for our loved ones or those coming to us for advice after suffering any type of trauma, it is helpful to remember the quote by Cheryl Richardson that I shared at the beginning of the book: *People start to heal the moment they feel heard.*

Also By Umm Zakiyyah

If I Should Speak
A Voice
Footsteps
Realities of Submission
Hearts We Lost
The Friendship Promise
Muslim Girl
His Other Wife
UZ Short Story Collection
The Test Paper (a children's book)
Pain. From the Journal of Umm Zakiyyah
Broken yet Faithful. From the Journal of Umm Zakiyyah
Faith. From the Journal of Umm Zakiyyah
Let's Talk About Sex and Muslim Love
Reverencing the Wombs That Broke You: A Daughter of Rape and Abuse Inspires Healing and Healthy Family
And Then I Gave Up: Essays About Faith and Spiritual Crisis in Islam
I Almost Left Islam: How I Reclaimed My Faith

Order information available at uzauthor.com/bookstore

Read more from Umm Zakiyyah at uzauthor.com

About the Author

Umm Zakiyyah is the bestselling author of the novels *If I Should Speak* trilogy, *Muslim Girl*, and *His Other Wife*; and the self-help book for religious survivors of abuse *Reverencing the Wombs That Broke You*. She writes about the interfaith struggles of Muslims and Christians and the intercultural, spiritual, and moral struggles of Muslims in America. Her work has earned praise from writers, professors, and filmmakers and has been translated into multiple languages.

Umm Zakiyyah holds a BA in elementary education and an MA in English language learning. She studied Arabic, Qur'an, Islamic sciences, *'aqeedah*, and *tafseer* in America, Egypt, and Saudi Arabia for more than fifteen years. She currently teaches *tajweed* (rules of reciting Qur'an) and *tafseer* in Baltimore, Maryland.

REFERENCES

Bedrick, D. (2014, September 25) 6 Reasons Not to Forgive, Not Yet. *PsychologyToday.com*. Retrieved July 4, 2017 from https://www.psychologytoday.com/blog/is-psychology-making-us-sick/201409/6-reasons-not-forgive-not-yet

Campbell, S. (2014, December 11) The 5 Faults With Forgiveness. *HuffingtonPost.com*. Retrieved July 9, 2017 from http://www.huffingtonpost.com/sherrie-campbell-phd/the-5-faults-with-forgive_b_6297338.html

Devega, C. (2015, August 23) Black America owes no forgiveness: How Christianity hinders racial justice. *Salon.com*. Retrieved July 1, 2017 from http://www.salon.com/2015/08/23/the_hypocrisy_of_black_forgiveness_partner/ Originally published via Alternet.org

Podrazik, J. (2013, March 7) Oprah On Forgiveness: This Definition Was 'Bigger Than An Aha Moment' (VIDEO) *HuffingtonPost.com*. Retrieved July 2, 2017 from http://www.huffingtonpost.com/2013/03/07/oprah-on-forgiveness-how-to-forgive_n_2821736.html

Polluck, A. (2016, January 20) Why I Don't Use the Word 'Forgiveness' in Trauma Therapy. *GoodTherapy.org*. Retrieved July 9, 2017 from http://www.goodtherapy.org/blog/why-i-dont-use-the-word-forgiveness-in-trauma-therapy-0120164

Springett, T. (nd) The Dangers of Repressing Your Anger. *Belief.net*. Retrieved July 2, 2017 from http://www.beliefnet.com/wellness/articles/the-dangers-of-repressing-your-anger.aspx

Tracy, N. (2016, May 26) Gaslighting Definition, Techniques And Being Gaslighted. *HealthyPlace.com*. Retrieved June 29, 2017 from https://www.healthyplace.com/abuse/emotional-psychological-abuse/gaslighting-definition-techniques-and-being-gaslighted/

Umm Zakiyyah (2016) *Faith. From the Journal of Umm Zakiyyah*. Camp Springs, MD: Al-Walaa Publications.

Umm Zakiyyah (2016) *Pain. From the Journal of Umm Zakiyyah*. Camp Springs, MD: Al-Walaa Publications.

Umm Zakiyyah, Davidson, M., & Banani, H. (2017) *Reverencing the Wombs That Broke You: A Daughter of Rape and Abuse Inspires Healing and Healthy Family*. Camp Springs, MD: Al-Walaa Publications.

Walker, P. (2015) *The Tao of Fully Feeling: Harvesting Forgiveness out of Blame*. Azure Coyote Publishing. Kindle. Retrieved from Amazon.com.

Made in the USA
Columbia, SC
29 May 2023

17484602R00069